English Unlimited

B1 Pre-intermediate
Self-study Pack (Workbook with DVD-ROM)

Maggie Baigent, Chris Cavey & Nick Robinson

CAMBRIDGE
UNIVERSITY PRESS

University Printing House, Cambridge CB2 8BS, United Kingdom

Cambridge University Press is part of the University of Cambridge.

It furthers the University's mission by disseminating knowledge in the pursuit of education, learning and research at the highest international levels of excellence.

www.cambridge.org
Information on this title: www.cambridge.org/9780521697781

First published 2010
6th printing 2014

Printed in Poland by Opolgraf

A catalogue record for this publication is available from the British Library

ISBN 978-0-521-69778-1 Pre-intermediate Self-study Pack (Workbook with DVD-ROM)
ISBN 978-0-521-69777-4 Pre-intermediate Coursebook with e-Portfolio
ISBN 978-0-521-69780-4 Pre-intermediate Teacher's Pack
ISBN 978-0-521-69779-8 Pre-intermediate Class Audio CDs

Contents

1 Play

1 Complete the words for different types of music.

Bonneville Music Festival
Music for everyone!

a p _o_ _p_

b c _ l _ p s _

c s _ _ _ s _

d h _ p - _ _ _ p

e r _ g g _ _ _

f c l a _ _ _ _ _ _ _ _ music

g f _ _ _ k music

2 Circle the correct words to complete what the people in the festival say about music.

1 We have a special instrument called / is the steel drum.   [b]

2 I was learned / brought up to play / sing classical music, but now I play guitar and sing in a band.

3 Our traditional / classical music is called folk.

4 I learned how / what to play the violin when I was little.

5 It's similar to / of a lot of music from Cuba; in fact, it's a mixture of Cuban and Puerto Rican dance music.

3 Match the sentences in Exercise 2 to the correct photos in Exercise 1.

VOCABULARY
Deciding what to do

Saturday 25th

18.00
Rumberos de Cuba
Dance music from Cuba

19.00
Rachid Taha
Rock with traditional Algerian rai influence

20.00
Children of Khmer
Classical Cambodian dance

21.00
Sharon Shannon Big Band
All-star ceilidh (traditional Irish dance)

22.00
Mor Karbasi
15th-century songs from Spain by this young female singer

4   Complete the conversation using the expressions in the box.

> have a look   Hang on   idea   not really into   see if
> sounds   that looks   think about   ~~want to~~

CONN   I was thinking about going to the festival on Saturday. **Do you** [1]___*want to*___ **go?**

RITA   It depends what's on. **Why don't we** [2]_____ at the programme?

CONN   OK. [3]_____ **a minute.** Right, **what do you** [4]_____ this – Children of Khmer?

RITA   Hm, I'm [5]_____ dance. What about Rachid Taha?

CONN   The Algerian music? Yes, [6]_____ **interesting.**

RITA   And the ceilidh [7]_____ **good,** too.

CONN   Yeah. **So do you want me to** [8]_____ there are any tickets?

RITA   **Good** [9]_____ .

VOCABULARY
Sports and exercise

5   Look at the pictures and complete the words.

1   r u_n_n_ing

2   s k _ i n g

3   y _ _ _

4   v _ _ _ _ _ _ b a l l

5   h _ _ _ _ _ _

6   k _ _ _ _ _ _

7   a e _ _ _ _ _ _ _

8   s w _ _ _ _ i n g

Over to you

Which sports do you like doing? Write three sentences.

6   Cross out the words that do *not* go with the verbs in bold.

1   **I play**   football / hockey / tennis / karate.
2   **I do**   yoga / aerobics / skiing / karate.
3   **I go**   swimming / skiing / boxing / running.

GRAMMAR

Present simple, past simple, present progressive

7 Read the introduction to the article and answer these questions.

1 Where did Wally work? 2 What does he do now?

8 Read the rest of the article quickly. What kind of music does Wally like?

An interview with Wally Cotgrave

Wally Cotgrave is 70 this year. He spent his working life in heavy industrial sites and petro-chemical plants. Then, at the age of 50, he decided to become a singer.

Interviewer Wally, were you always interested in music?

Wally Well, when I was a child, I loved all the Hollywood musicals, and I learned all the songs by watching the films again and again.

Interviewer But how did you get into singing seriously?

Wally Well, I was a terrible singer! People always told me to stop, but I couldn't – I just loved singing. Then, when I was about 50, we moved out of London to a small town with a very active musical group.

I wanted to sing with them, so I had lessons with a brilliant teacher.

Interviewer What kind of music do you sing?

Wally I love all the songs of the 1940s and '50s, but I mostly sing in musicals with the local group.

Interviewer How many shows have you been in?

Wally Oh, too many to remember! But I had solo parts in *Oliver!* and *My Fair Lady*. And I was on TV once for about ten seconds in a talent show!

Interviewer So, how often do you sing these days?

Wally Every day!

Interviewer And are you working on anything special at the moment?

Wally Well, the next show is *Hello, Dolly!*, and there's a solo part for an older man, so I'm preparing for that. I hope I get it!

Interviewer What would you say to someone who wants to sing?

Wally If I can do it, everybody can!

9 Complete the questions about Wally using the verbs in brackets in the correct form. Use the present simple, past simple or present progressive.

1 How __*did*__ Wally __*learn*__ songs when he was young? (learn)

2 _____ he _____ a good voice when he was younger? (have)

3 Why _____ he _____ to have singing lessons? (decide)

4 What kind of music _____ Wally _____? (sing)

5 Who _____ he usually _____ with? (sing)

6 _____ Wally _____ every day? (sing)

7 What _____ he _____ at the moment? (do)

10 Read the article again and write the answers to the questions in Exercise 9.

TimeOut

11 Read these sentences about strange sports. Are they true or false?

1 Octopush is the sport of underwater hockey.   TRUE / FALSE
2 If you zorb, you go down a hill inside a giant ball.   TRUE / FALSE
3 In disc golf, the players throw CDs into a basket.   TRUE / FALSE
4 Chessboxing is a combination of chess and boxing.   TRUE / FALSE
5 In korfball, the players try to put a ball in a *korf*.   TRUE / FALSE

12 Which sports sound the most interesting to you? Tick the ones you would like to try.

EXPLORE Reading

13 Look at the web page for the Summer School and write the questions (1–6) in the correct spaces (a–f).

1 What about the social life?
2 ~~What is the Glamorgan Summer School?~~
3 Is there any accommodation?
4 What about off-campus?
5 What courses are on offer?
6 Who can come?

14 Are the sentences true or false?

1	There is good public transport to the university campus.	(TRUE)/ FALSE
2	At the end of every course, you get a qualification.	TRUE / FALSE
3	There are a lot of things to do in Cardiff.	TRUE / FALSE
4	There is no accommodation on campus.	TRUE / FALSE

15 (Circle) the correct meaning of the underlined expressions on the web page. Guess if you are not sure.

1 a it's very expensive
  (b it's not very expensive)
2 a people who like walking
  b people with different experience
3 a people with children can go to the Summer School
  b people with children can go to the sports camp
4 a there are a lot of different courses
  b you can only find these courses on the Summer School
5 a there are a lot of different types of entertainment
  b you can eat a lot of different types of food
6 a all the accommodation is in hotel suites
  b all the rooms have private bathrooms

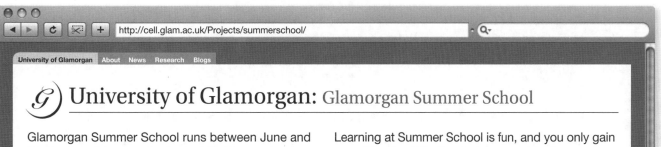

http://cell.glam.ac.uk/Projects/summerschool/

University of Glamorgan | About | News | Research | Blogs

𝒢 University of Glamorgan: Glamorgan Summer School

Glamorgan Summer School runs between June and September. It is an annual event that began over 100 years ago, offering a wide range of taster, day and week-long residential courses.

a *What is the Glamorgan Summer School?*

It is an Adult Education Summer School which gives you the opportunity to learn new skills and to meet people. It's held at the University of Glamorgan, and we're easy to get to by car and public transport. Most of all, it's [1]great value for money, it's friendly – and it's fun!

b _____

Are you over 18? Then you're welcome. We welcome students of all ages and abilities and [2]from all walks of life – qualifications don't matter. We welcome people with learning disabilities, and provide a playscheme and sports camp so [3]parents don't miss out.

c _____

The programme of courses is [4]really varied – Music, Mosaic, Photography, Tai Chi and more!

Learning at Summer School is fun, and you only gain a qualification if that's what you want to do.

d _____

We have lots of free social and cultural entertainment provided by a variety of different groups, with [5]something for every taste. There are discos, concerts, talks and workshops, not forgetting nightly jazz sessions performed by our jazz tutors and their students.

e _____

We are just eight miles from Cardiff, the capital of Wales and a city alive with culture and great nightlife – just a short bus or train ride away. Locally, there are numerous places of historical and cultural interest – and the Brecon Beacons National Park is only a short drive away.

f _____

Students at the Summer School can stay in the excellent [6]en-suite accommodation on the University campus.

1 Before you watch, think about this question: what games or sports did you do when you were young? Do you still do the same things now?

2 Watch the video and match the photos (1–3) with the activities (a–c).

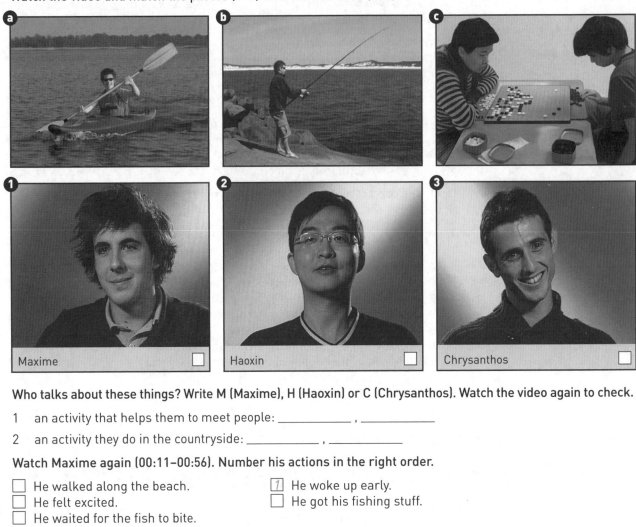

a

b

c

1 Maxime ☐

2 Haoxin ☐

3 Chrysanthos ☐

3 Who talks about these things? Write M (Maxime), H (Haoxin) or C (Chrysanthos). Watch the video again to check.

1 an activity that helps them to meet people: _____ , _____

2 an activity they do in the countryside: _____ , _____

4 Watch Maxime again (00:11–00:56). Number his actions in the right order.

☐ He walked along the beach.
☐ He felt excited.
☐ He waited for the fish to bite.

[1] He woke up early.
☐ He got his fishing stuff.

5 Watch Haoxin again (01:00–01:38). Complete the information about the game that he describes.

The ancient game of *Go* started [1] *two thousand* years ago. The rules are simple: the players place [2]_____ and [3]_____ stones on a board, which is divided into [4]_____ by [5]_____ squares. The aim of the game is to control a [6]_____ part of the board than the other player.

6 Watch Chrysanthos again (01:42–02:44). Are the sentences true or false?

1 Chrysanthos's brother and sister went rowing at weekends.   TRUE / FALSE
2 Chrysanthos didn't want to go at first.   TRUE / FALSE
3 Chrysanthos didn't like doing any sports.   TRUE / FALSE
4 He didn't like the place or the people where his brother and sister went.   TRUE / FALSE
5 He started kayaking because it was better for his body shape.   TRUE / FALSE

7 Have you tried any of these or any similar activities? Would you like to?

GLOSSARY

stuff (noun): an informal word for *things*
bite (verb): If a fish **bites** when you are fishing, it takes the food or hook in its mouth.
ancient (adjective): very, very old
grid (noun): straight lines that form squares on, for example, paper or a board
board (noun): a square piece of wood or card that you play a game on
rowing /ˈrəʊɪŋ/ (noun): the activity of moving a small kind of boat with no motor ⟶

2 Work and studies

1 Cross out the word in each group that is *not* correct.

1 I did a course / a subject / a degree in archaeology.
2 I applied to Art College / School / degree.
3 I studied science / maths / exams.
4 I'm writing a thesis / an exam / an essay.
5 I enjoyed the course / a degree / the subject.
6 I passed the college / exam / course.
7 I got a doctorate / an exam / a degree in biology.
8 I went to university / school / studies in the United States.

2 Complete what the people say about their studies with the present perfect of the verbs in brackets. Remember to put the adverbs in the correct position.

1 I *'ve never been* good at maths. (never/be)

2 It's the most difficult subject I _____. (ever/study)

3 I _____ studying alone. (always/enjoy)

4 I _____ a lot of exams in my life. (do)

5 I _____ an essay in English. (never/write)

6 I _____ several part-time courses. (do)

7 She's the best teacher I _____ . (ever/have)

8 I _____ an exam. (never/fail)

VOCABULARY

Working
conditions

3 Complete the magazine article using the words and expressions in the box.

at home   atmosphere   ~~benefits~~   easy   flexible   holiday
management   part-time   pay   place   stressful

Working life
Today, Naseema Bradley talks about her work

I studied accountancy at university, then went to work in the health service as an administration officer. The ¹ _benefits_ were good – we had five weeks' ² _____ and a private pension plan – but I wasn't happy in my job. The ³ _____ wasn't great – I never had any money at the end of the month! – and the work was very ⁴ _____ .

Then, after 15 years, our department closed, and I lost my job. It seemed like a disaster, but in fact, it saved my life! After two months, I found a job in a small office. It's a much nicer ⁵ _____ to work. We have ⁶ _____ working hours, and there's a nice ⁷ _____ in the office. The ⁸ _____ and my colleagues are very ⁹ _____ to work with. And the best thing about it is that it's ¹⁰ _____ – three days a week. So I can also do some work ¹¹ _____ – I advise people about tax and do their accounts. I work hard, but I organise my own life now and I'm much happier.

Over to you

What are the working conditions like in your present or past job? Write three sentences.

GRAMMAR

The present perfect 2 – with *for* and *since*

4 Complete the sentences using the verbs in the box in the present perfect and *for* or *since*.

be   be   ~~have~~   know   like   live   play   work

1   They _have had_ the same car _for_ ten years.

2   I _____ my boyfriend _____ the 1990s.

3   He _____ a teacher _____ more than 30 years.

4   She _____ for this company _____ a month.

5   We _____ in this flat _____ last April.

6   I _____ science _____ I studied it at primary school.

7   She _____ the guitar _____ she was 12.

8   He _____ with the same company _____ nearly 12 years.

Presenting
yourself

5 Complete this extract from an application letter with the correct prepositions. Be careful – one expression does not need a preposition!

and I am now **looking** [1] _for_ **work** in Human Resources.

As you can see from my CV, I **have a degree** [2] _____ **business studies** and **a diploma** [3] _____ **marketing**. I **have experience** [4] _____ **marketing** and **have been** [5] _____ **PR** for about two years now.

I **enjoy** [6] _____ **working** in a team and **am good** [7] _____ **working** under pressure. I have always **wanted** [8] _____ **work** for a large company and

MYEnglish

6 Read what these people say about using English at work. Are these sentences true or false?

1 Lyudmila doesn't speak English very often. TRUE / FALSE
2 Kamal has difficulty using technical English. TRUE / FALSE
3 Marisa only speaks English when she goes to England. TRUE / FALSE

I make phone calls in English to my colleagues abroad nearly every day.

I only use technical language for my work, so I have difficulty with everyday conversation in English, for example when we go out for dinner with clients.

I use English to communicate with our customers in Japan and China.

Lyudmila, Ukraine

Kamal, Sudan

Marisa, Portugal

Your English

7 Do you use English like these people? Complete the language profile for you.

How do you use English in your job? If you're not working, how would you like to use English in the future?

Tick (✓) one or more, or write your answer.

Making phone calls ☐

Speaking to people face to face ☐

Reading and writing emails and letters ☐

Writing reports and presentations ☐

Other _____

I never use English at work. ☐

Where have you studied English?

At school or university ☐

I've done courses at a language school. ☐

I've had in-company English training. ☐

I've done a course in an English-speaking country. ☐

Other _____

I've never studied English properly. ☐

What would be useful for you to improve your English?

Regular English lessons (e.g. one or two a week) ☐

Short courses on specific skills (e.g. telephone English, writing emails) ☐

An intensive (full immersion) course for a week ☐

Other _____

If possible, show your profile to your teacher, and ask for their suggestions to improve your English skills.

EXPLOREWriting

8 Read this announcement from a company magazine. Are the sentences true or false?

1 Anyone who works for the company can apply for this opportunity. TRUE / FALSE
2 The company will only pay for the English lessons. TRUE / FALSE

WIN a two-week English course!

Applications in English by email to Simone Lidowski, HR Department, manager.hr@uniton.com

Uniton is offering FIVE of its employees the chance to attend a two-week English course in the UK or United States, with all expenses, including flights and accommodation, paid.

---

9 Read the email of application. The <u>underlined</u> phrases are inappropriate or too informal. Replace them with phrases from the box.

> advertised
> Dear Ms Lidowski
> I enjoy
> I have difficulty in
> I have studied
> I have worked
> I would like
> improve my spoken English
> project the company's image effectively
> Regards

Dear Ms Lidowski ——— ¹<u>Hi</u>

²<u>I want</u> to apply for the English course ³<u>you talked about</u> in the recent company newsletter. ⁴<u>I've been</u> in the export department for two years and I use English every day. In addition, ⁵<u>I've done</u> English in a private language school to try and improve my level.

⁶<u>I really like</u> communicating by email, but ⁷<u>I'm not very good at</u> speaking to customers on the phone. A course in the USA would ⁸<u>make my spoken English better</u> and help me to ⁹<u>make the company look good</u>.

¹⁰<u>Love</u>
R. Schultz

10 Write your application for the opportunity in Exercise 8. Include information from your language profile (Exercise 7) and use a polite, formal style.

1 Before you watch, think about this question: have you ever gone to classes to learn something in your free time? What kind of things did you learn?

2 Watch the video and ⟨circle⟩ the correct way to complete the sentences.

Mainda   Paivi

1 Mainda went to acting classes to …
  a) start a new career.
  b) improve her confidence.
  c) meet people.
2 Paivi went to dance classes to …
  a) meet people.
  b) become a dance teacher.
  c) learn more about salsa.

3 Watch Mainda again (00:13–00:55) and match the beginnings and endings of the phrases.

1 I took some introductory   a) voice exercises.
2 The acting classes concentrated on b) mooing like cows.
3 There were a lot of   c) type of acting classes.
4 We did things like   d) was about.
5 That's what the training   e) voice projection.

4 Are the sentences about Paivi's classes true or false? Watch again (01:01–02:06) to check.

1 Paivi went to the classes before and after her trip to Cuba.   TRUE / FALSE
2 There was space for about 30 people in the classes.   TRUE / FALSE
3 They had to go with a partner.   TRUE / FALSE
4 They learned about South American and Cuban dance music.   TRUE / FALSE
5 There was a friendly atmosphere in the classes.   TRUE / FALSE

5 Paivi uses the same word in both phrases in each pair. Can you guess what the words are? Watch again to check.

1 you could fit about 20 _people_ there

  you met lots of _people_, both women and men

2 when we came _____ from Cuba

  I went _____ to the classes

3 I _____ wanted to continue

  it was a _____ great place

4 we just learned _____ _____ dancing

  I learned _____ _____ about music

5 the _____ who you meet

  you get _____ from all walks of life

6 Which of these classes would you prefer to go to? Why?

GLOSSARY

moo (verb): make a sound like a cow
role-playing (noun): an activity where you 'act' a situation
got the salsa bug: If you **get the bug** for something, you become very enthusiastic about it.
fit (verb): If you can **fit** something in a place, there is enough space for it.
from all walks of life: people of many different types

3

How's your food?

1 Look at the word snake and find five more adjectives to describe shops.

endioldfashionedstendemptylonefriendlyismatconvenientortheexpensivepeatnoisyarnted

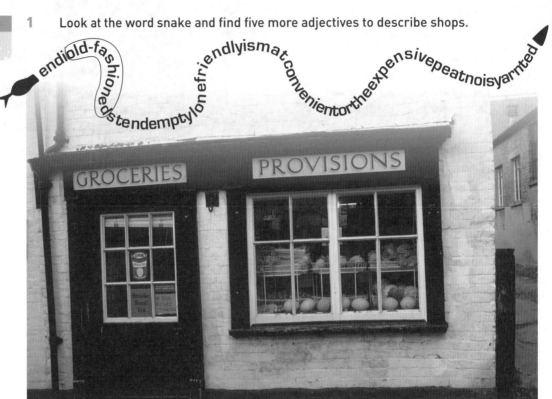

2 Add the vowels to these adjectives. Then match them with their opposites from Exercise 1.

1 <u>u</u> n f r <u>i</u> <u>e</u> n d l y   *friendly*

2 m _ d _ r n   _____

3 c h _ _ p   _____

4 _ n c _ n v _ n _ _ n t   _____

5 q _ _ _ t   _____

6 c r _ w d _ d   _____

3 Use some of the adjectives from Exercises 1 and 2 to complete what Patricia says about shopping.

The market where I buy my fruit and vegetables is always very busy.
It's ¹ c *rowded* and ² n_____ , but the people are always very
³ f_____ , and the food is fresh and ⁴ c_____ . It's also very
⁵ c_____ because it's only five minutes from where I live.

Patricia, Spain

Over to you

Write a few
sentences about
how you like to
shop. Use some of
the adjectives from
Exercises 1 and 2.

4 Who says it? The waiter (W) or the customer (C)?

1 And for you? `W`
2 Anything to drink? ☐
3 Are you ready to order? ☐
4 Can we have the bill, please? ☐
5 Sparkling or still? ☐
6 Could we have a bottle of water, please? ☐
7 Yes. I'll have the soup, please. ☐
8 Me too, please – soup. ☐
9 No problem, come this way, please. ☐
10 No, is there a table for two? ☐
11 Of course, I'll bring it for you. ☐
12 Still, please. And two glasses. ☐

5 Now use the sentences from Exercise 4 to complete the dialogues.

Arriving

WAITER   Good evening. Do you have a reservation?

CUSTOMER ¹ *No, is there a table for two?*

WAITER   ² _____

Ordering

WAITER   ³ _____

CUSTOMER Yes. I'll have the soup, please.

WAITER   ⁴ _____

CUSTOMER ⁵ _____

WAITER   ⁶ _____

CUSTOMER ⁷ _____

WAITER   ⁸ _____

CUSTOMER Still, please. And two glasses.

Paying

CUSTOMER ⁹ _____

WAITER   Of course. I'll bring it for you.

6 Make prepositional phrases from the box to complete the sentences.
Use each phrase only once.

noun	preposition	phrase
~~table~~	with	the corner
meal	in	~~two~~
chicken	for	garlic sauce
bottle	of	red wine
menu		lots of vegetarian dishes
table		25 people

1 Hello. Could I book a *table for two* for eight thirty, please?

2 To drink, we'll have a _____, please.

3 Do you want to be next to the window, or would you like the _____?

4 I recommend the _____. It's very tasty!

5 I'm cooking a _____ on Saturday – my whole family!

6 There's a good _____ for people who don't eat meat.

3

7 Cross out the expression that is *not* possible.

1 How about / What about / ~~Why don't we~~ some pasta?
2 Perhaps we should / Why don't we / What about get some ice cream?
3 We can / We could / How about put some sausages on the barbecue.
4 What about / What should / What can we make for dessert?
5 Why don't we / How about / We can make a salad for the vegetarians.
6 How about / What should / What about burgers?

TimeOut

8 Read the sentences and circle the numbers that are true for you. 1 = Disagree strongly; 5 = Agree strongly

1	I find supermarkets quite stressful.	1 2 3 4 5
2	Small shops are better, even if things cost more.	1 2 3 4 5
3	Shopping in supermarkets is bad for the environment.	1 2 3 4 5
4	I think supermarkets are crowded and noisy.	1 2 3 4 5
5	Supermarkets are only interested in making money.	1 2 3 4 5

Now add up your total score.

5–11 You like to shop in a place that's cheap and convenient. Why shop in small shops when you can find everything you want in one place?

12–18 You think that supermarkets are unfriendly and bad for the environment, but they make shopping so easy.

19–25 Small shops give you everything you want – great food and friendly service. You hardly ever go to a supermarket.

9 Complete the crossword.

EXPLORE**Reading**

10 Match the sentences (1–4) with the correct heading (a–d).

a Cost b Food c Service d Setting

1 The steak was perfect, but the rice was a bit undercooked.
2 The staff are young, but very good – they did a great job.
3 The total price was $190 for three of us, which is quite expensive.
4 It's dark and quiet – the perfect place for a romantic meal for two.

11 Read the reviews. Match the restaurants (1–4) with the food (a–d).

a chicken curry c paella
b lasagne and green salad d Middle Eastern food

---

www.mealsout.co.nz

| Reviews | Add a review |

1 El Buho Azul Murray Street   *Review by: mayfly*

I love El Buho Azul. The food is fantastic, the service is very fast, and the staff are lovely. It's not the most beautiful place in the world, but I don't go to restaurants to look around – I go to eat! And El Buho Azul has the best paella in Wellington. The menu is all Spanish. It's not very good for vegetarians, as most dishes are meat or seafood.

2 Bella Napoli William Street   *Review by: Jorge*

A high-class restaurant with truly excellent food – but don't come here if you like to eat a lot but not pay a lot. It's *very* expensive. The menu is modern Italian – pizzas, pastas and some interesting salads – and the service was very good. All in all, this is the perfect restaurant when you want to go somewhere special and spend a little bit extra.

3 Cedar Tree Parker Avenue   *Review by: PeeCee*

I love Lebanese food, but I was a bit disappointed with the Cedar Tree. The food was not the problem – it was all very good (but the portions were a bit small – I was still hungry after my meal). The big problem was that everything was very slow – we waited more than 45 minutes for our main course. The Cedar Tree is the best place in town for Lebanese food – but don't go there if you want a quick meal!

4 The Taj Percival Street   *Review by: Stroller*

We go to The Taj about once a week. It's cheap, we love the food, and – best of all – the staff love children. My kids are seven and four and they love it when we go to The Taj. The menu has a really wide range of Indian dishes that are very tasty – and very cheap. It's sometimes very noisy – especially when my children are there!

---

12 Look at what these people say and decide which restaurant is best for them.

It's my dad's birthday, and I want to take him somewhere special. Money is not a problem!

Pete

Ravi

I want to go out for a family meal, but I don't want to spend a lot of money. My husband is vegetarian, but our daughter and I eat meat.

Sonia

Over to you

Write a website review for a restaurant you know.

I want somewhere I can have a quick meal before going to the cinema. I don't want somewhere too high class – just quick and tasty. And I want somewhere with good seafood – I don't eat meat.

1   Before you watch, thin about this question: what do you like to cook? How do you make your favourite food?

2   Look at this list of ingredients. Watch the video and tick (✓) the ones that Nilgun and Alex mention.

almonds	✓	ginger	☐
anchovies	☐	monkey nuts	☐
beef	☐	onions	☐
chicken	☐	pistachios	☐
chilli	☐	potatoes	☐
coconut rice	☐	salmon	☐
garlic	☐	spring onions	☐

3   Nilgun talks about *lokum*, and Alex talks about *nasi lemak*. Which food is each sentence about?
    Write L (*lokum*) or N (*nasi lemak*).

Nilgun

lokum

Alex

nasi lemak

1   It's sweet. _____

2   It's made with rice. _____

3   It tastes better than it sounds. _____

4   Some kinds are made with nuts. _____

4   Look at what Nilgun says about Haci Bekir, the inventor of *lokum*, and ⓒircle the correct answers.
    Watch again (00:11–01:00) to check.

He ¹has / had a factory in Istanbul many many years ago and he ²becomes / became so famous and he ³opens / opened all these little shops.

5   Look at what Alex says about why he likes cooking and ⓒircle the correct answers.
    Watch again (01:05–02:13) to check.

Cooking ¹is / was a way for me to de-stress myself, so after a long day at work, I ²come / came back and then I ³cook / cooked.

6   What tense does Nilgun mostly use? What tense does Alex mostly use? Why?

7   What is a typical dish from your country? What is it made from? How do you make it?

GLOSSARY

factory (noun): a place where things are made
de-stress (verb): If you **de-stress** yourself, you relax and get away from all the stressful things in your life.
anchovy (noun): a small, very salty fish
pistachios / almonds / monkey nuts (nouns): different kinds of nut

4 Encounters

VOCABULARY
Taxis

1 Complete this section from a guide to Milan, Italy, using the words in the box.

change   fare   meter   passengers   receipt   ~~taxi rank~~   tip

GETTING AROUND
Taxis

Milan

In Milan, you can phone for a taxi or get one at a ¹ _taxi rank_ .
Most of them are normal cars and can take four ² _____ , but
there are bigger taxis for more people or disabled passengers. All
drivers use a ³ _____ , and you pay the exact ⁴ _____ at
the end of your journey. The driver will always give you the correct
⁵ _____ , and people don't usually give a ⁶ _____ . If you
need a ⁷ _____ , just ask the driver before you pay.

Over to you

Write some
information about
taxis for visitors to
your town.

VOCABULARY
Getting a taxi

2 For each of these sentences, decide who's speaking – the taxi driver (T) or
the passenger (P).

1   Just make it 30 dollars.   [P]
2   Have a good trip, then.   [ ]
3   Can you take me to Terminal 2, please?   [ ]
4   So, is this your first time in Sydney?   [ ]
5   Can I have a receipt, please?   [ ]
6   How much is it to the airport?   [ ]
7   That's $27.80, please.   [ ]
8   Can I put my bags in the back?   [ ]

3 Complete the conversation using six of the sentences in Exercise 2.

PASSENGER	Hello. ¹ _____
TAXI DRIVER	Well, it depends on the traffic, but it's usually about 25 to 30 dollars.
PASSENGER	OK, that's fine. ² _____
TAXI DRIVER	I'll do it for you.
PASSENGER	Thanks. ³ _____
✳✳✳	
TAXI DRIVER	Here we are. Terminal 2. ⁴ _____
PASSENGER	Sorry, I've only got $100. And ⁵ _____
TAXI DRIVER	Sure. ⁶ _____
PASSENGER	Thanks. Bye.

4 Complete this New York taxi story using the time expressions in the box.

After   During   ~~later~~   then   When

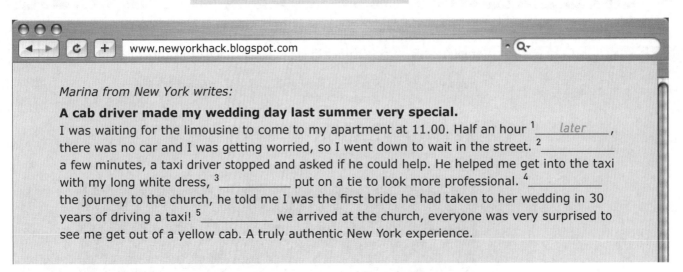

Marina from New York writes:

A cab driver made my wedding day last summer very special.
I was waiting for the limousine to come to my apartment at 11.00. Half an hour ¹____*later*____, there was no car and I was getting worried, so I went down to wait in the street. ²_____ a few minutes, a taxi driver stopped and asked if he could help. He helped me get into the taxi with my long white dress, ³_____ put on a tie to look more professional. ⁴_____ the journey to the church, he told me I was the first bride he had taken to her wedding in 30 years of driving a taxi! ⁵_____ we arrived at the church, everyone was very surprised to see me get out of a yellow cab. A truly authentic New York experience.

5 Read this email to a taxi firm, and circle the correct verb forms.

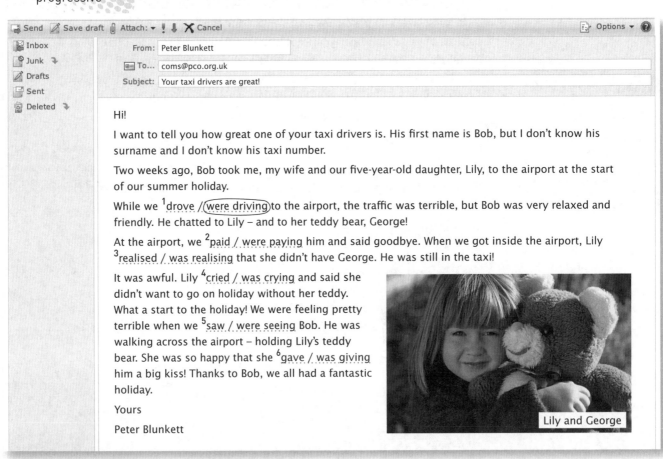

Send   Save draft   Attach: Cancel   Options

Inbox
Junk
Drafts
Sent
Deleted

From: Peter Blunkett
To... coms@pco.org.uk
Subject: Your taxi drivers are great!

Hi!

I want to tell you how great one of your taxi drivers is. His first name is Bob, but I don't know his surname and I don't know his taxi number.

Two weeks ago, Bob took me, my wife and our five-year-old daughter, Lily, to the airport at the start of our summer holiday.

While we ¹drove /(were driving)to the airport, the traffic was terrible, but Bob was very relaxed and friendly. He chatted to Lily – and to her teddy bear, George!

At the airport, we ²paid / were paying him and said goodbye. When we got inside the airport, Lily ³realised / was realising that she didn't have George. He was still in the taxi!

It was awful. Lily ⁴cried / was crying and said she didn't want to go on holiday without her teddy. What a start to the holiday! We were feeling pretty terrible when we ⁵saw / were seeing Bob. He was walking across the airport – holding Lily's teddy bear. She was so happy that she ⁶gave / was giving him a big kiss! Thanks to Bob, we all had a fantastic holiday.

Yours

Peter Blunkett

Lily and George

6 Complete the sentences for starting a story using *for*, *in*, *to*, *with* or – (no preposition).

1   I was living ___*in*___ Caracas.
2   I was going _____ Mexico.
3   I was working _____ a bar.
4   I was travelling _____ Europe.
5   I was visiting _____ Hong Kong.

6   I was waiting _____ my flight.
7   I was _____ some friends.
8   I was looking _____ a hostel.
9   I was on my way _____ the airport.
10 It was _____ winter, and very cold.

MYEnglish

7 Read what these people say in the *Cambridge Encyclopedia of Language*. Match them with their reasons for learning English (a–e).

When I finish learning English, my pay as secretary will increase by nearly ten times.

1 trainee secretary, Egypt

My company plans big deals with the Arabic world. None of us speak Arabic, and they do not know Japanese. All our plans and meetings are in English.

2 businessman, Japan

Nearly everyone in Denmark speaks English. If we didn't, there wouldn't be anyone to talk to.

After I learned English, I felt I was in touch with the international world for the very first time.

4 doctor, India

3 teacher, Nigeria

If I want to keep up to date with the latest techniques and products, I must certainly maintain my English very strongly.

5 university student, Denmark

I need English ...
a ... to feel I am part of the global community.   3
b ... to learn about new things in my job.   ☐
c ... for communicating in my work.   ☐
d ... because my language is not spoken outside my country.   ☐
e ... to have more money.   ☐

8 Look at sentences a–e in Exercise 7 and match the sentence halves to complete the rules.

1 We use *to* ...
2 We use *for* ...
3 We use *because* ...

a ... to join two sentences.
b ... before an infinitive verb.
c ... before an *–ing* verb.

9 Complete these other reasons for learning English with *to*, *for* or *because*.

I learn English ...

1 __to__ read books or magazines about things I'm interested in.

2 _____ I like watching films in the original language.

3 _____ improve my chances of getting a good job.

4 _____ chatting with people on the Internet.

5 _____ a lot of my favourite musicians sing in English.

6 _____ I attend international meetings and conferences.

7 _____ writing emails to colleagues and clients.

8 _____ communicate with people when I travel.

YourEnglish

10 Why are you learning English? Tick the reasons in Exercises 7 and 9 that are true for you, and add any other reasons.

EXPLORE**Writing**

11 Read this email to a taxi firm and choose the correct reason why Rosa is writing.

    a   to complain about something
    b   to ask for help

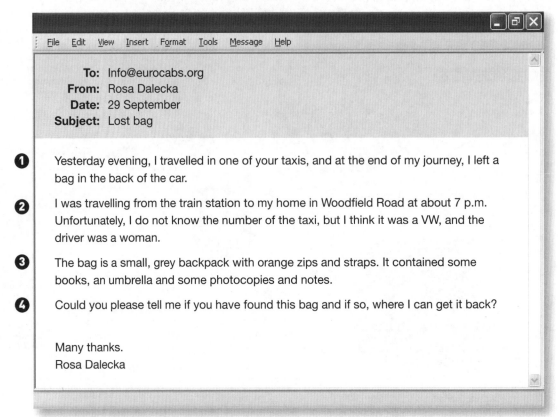

To: Info@eurocabs.org
From: Rosa Dalecka
Date: 29 September
Subject: Lost bag

❶ Yesterday evening, I travelled in one of your taxis, and at the end of my journey, I left a bag in the back of the car.

❷ I was travelling from the train station to my home in Woodfield Road at about 7 p.m. Unfortunately, I do not know the number of the taxi, but I think it was a VW, and the driver was a woman.

❸ The bag is a small, grey backpack with orange zips and straps. It contained some books, an umbrella and some photocopies and notes.

❹ Could you please tell me if you have found this bag and if so, where I can get it back?

Many thanks.
Rosa Dalecka

12 Which paragraph of the email ...

    a   asks for information?   ☐
    b   gives details of the bag?   ☐
    c   describes the problem?   ☐
    d   gives details of the taxi journey?   ☐

13 Choose words from the table or add other words to describe a bag you use.

	small	black	plastic	backpack		wheels.
It's a	medium	red	leather	shopping bag	with	straps.
	big	brown	cotton	bag		a zip.

14 Imagine you left your bag in a taxi. Write an email to the taxi company. Don't forget to:

- say when and where you were travelling
- describe the bag and what is in it
- ask where you can get it back.

1 Before you watch, try to complete this table.

Country	Nationality	Main languages
1 _Switzerland_	Swiss	German, 2_____ and Italian
Japan	3_____	4_____
5_____	Afghan	Pashto and Dari
6_____	Indian	Hindi and English

2 The missing words from Exercise 1 are all in the video. What do you think Lona talks about? Watch the video and check your answers in the table.

Lona

3 Watch the video again. Use words from the table in Exercise 1 to complete these sentences about Lona's encounter.

1 Lona was in _____ at the time.

2 The man she met was _____ . His wife was _____ .

3 The man was wearing traditional _____ clothes.

4 Lona and the man spoke in _____ first, then in _____ .

5 The man's wife also spoke _____ and _____ as second languages.

6 The man had travelled in _____ and _____ .

7 Lona and the man also chatted in _____ .

4 Lona uses a lot of adjectives to describe her experience. Use the adjectives in the box to complete these phrases from the video. Watch again to check.

> beautiful   beautiful   little   ~~magnificent~~   nice   unusual

1 There's a _magnificent_ lake, which is very _____ .

2 There was one family that looked very _____ .

3 He was wearing something that seemed quite _____ .

4 They had two _____ kids.

5 That was a very _____ experience.

5 Watch again and (circle) the words that Lona uses to say why this was an interesting encounter.

It was just like a complete 1(mix)/ mixture of culture, and for me that 2man / family demonstrated an acceptance of 3different / several cultures and they had 4really / actually incorporated different cultures into their 5lives / lifestyle.

6 Have you ever had a similar multicultural or multilingual encounter?

GLOSSARY

loose-fitting (adjective): **Loose-fitting** clothes are comfortable and not tight.
robe (noun): a type of long dress worn by both men and women
pointy (adjective): **Pointy** shoes have a point at the toes.
turban (noun): a long piece of cloth which is worn wrapped around the head
acceptance (noun): If you **accept** something (or show **an acceptance** of something), it has become normal for you.
incorporated into: included, or made a part of something

Money

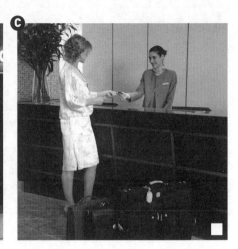

1 Look at the conversations in Exercises 2–4 and write the correct numbers on the photos.

2 Number the conversation in the correct order.

___ Sorry, do you have any smaller notes?

_1_ Hello. Can I change these euros into Canadian dollars, please?

___ Sure. Are twenties OK?

___ Of course. That's 50, 100, 150, 200 euros. So that's $332.22. Here you are.

___ Fine. Thanks.

3 Complete the conversation using the words in the box.

bill   cards   pay   PIN   receipt

A Could I have the ^{1}_____bill_____, please? Room 13.

B Certainly. How would you like to ^{2}_____?

A Do you take ^{3}_____?

B Yes, we do. Just a moment. Can you type in your ^{4}_____, please?

A Sure.

B That's fine, and here's your ^{5}_____.

4 Put the words in the correct order to complete the conversation.

A OK. That's one day return ticket to Cardiff. ^{1}to / you / How / like / pay / would / ?

B Sorry, ^{2}is / how / much / it / ?

A £13.80.

B OK, ^{3}cash / in / pay / I'll / .

A ^{4}have / you / smaller / Do / anything / ?

B Sorry, no. That's all I've got.

5 Match 1–5 with a–e.

1 Can I get a student ticket?

2 Do I have to book my ticket in advance?

3 Can I pay by card?

4 I have to change some dollars.

5 Sorry, we can't accept euros.

a No, sorry. You have to pay in cash.

b Yes, but you have to show your student card.

c Oh, OK. Can I pay by card?

d No, you don't have to do that, but it's a good idea.

e You can do that in the hotel.

VOCABULARY
Giving advice

6 Circle the correct expressions to complete the advice and rules for visitors to these places.

1 You don't have to / can't take photos.
2 You can / shouldn't smoke here.
3 You don't have to / can't pay if you live here.
4 You should / don't have to switch off your mobile.
5 Don't / You don't have to drive your car here.
6 You don't have to / shouldn't wear shoes.
7 You can / shouldn't take glasses out of the pub.
8 You don't have to / should put your books back.
9 You shouldn't / have to leave things in your room.
10 Don't / You have to show your ticket here.

TimeOut

7 Complete the crossword with money words.

ACROSS

2 You have to pay your electricity, gas and water ___bills___.
4 This is the official money in a country, e.g. euros or dollars.
5 You can get money from a bank or a _____ machine.
6 This type of money is made of metal.
7 If you use your card to pay, you usually need this number.
8 The euro has _____ of 500, 200, 100, 50, 20, 10 and 5.

DOWN

1 This is the money used in the USA, Canada, Australia and other countries.
2 You can pay for things in cash or _____ card.
3 When you buy something, you usually get a _____.
4 When you arrive in a country, you can _____ money at the airport.

Crossword: 2 Across: B I L L S

EXPLOREReading

8   Look at the travel web page opposite giving advice for people going to India. Tick (✓) the money services that are mentioned.

1 banks   ✓
2 cash machines   ☐
3 traveller's cheques   ☐
4 credit cards   ☐
5 private money changers   ☐
6 airport exchange banks   ☐
7 international money transfers   ☐
8 cash advances (getting cash with your credit card)   ☐
9 hotel exchange desks   ☐

9   Read the information on the web page and decide if these tips are good or bad advice.

Money tips - India

1 It's a good idea to always have some cash with you.	GOOD / BAD
2 Leave your passport in the hotel; you don't need it to change money.	GOOD / BAD
3 Take your card – you'll find an ATM in every town and village.	GOOD / BAD
4 Don't keep the emergency lost-and-stolen phone numbers with your credit card.	GOOD / BAD
5 Take US or Australian dollars; you can change these everywhere.	GOOD / BAD
6 Remember to change your rupees before you leave India.	GOOD / BAD
7 Don't go to private money changers.	GOOD / BAD
8 You should take traveller's cheques in pounds sterling or US dollars.	GOOD / BAD

10 Look at the <u>underlined</u> words on the web page. They can have more than one meaning. Which meaning is correct here?

1 denominations
  a the values or units of coins or banknotes
  b different types of Christianity
2 backup
  a a copy of data on a computer
  b something extra which you can use if you need
3 maintain
  a always have with you
  b repair regularly to keep in good condition
4 leftover
  a not used
  b not eaten
5 wire
  a connect a piece of electrical equipment
  b send money electronically
6 proof-of-purchase slip
  a a receipt from a shop to show you have bought something
  b a receipt from a bank to show you have changed money

Over to you

Write some money tips for people visiting your country.

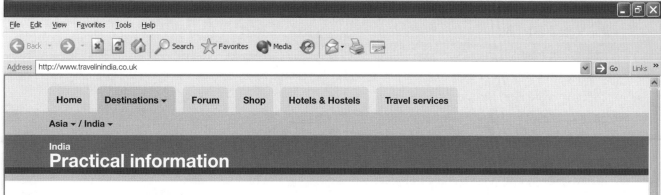

File   Edit   View   Favorites   Tools   Help

Back   ·   ·   Search   Favorites   Media

Address   http://www.travelinindia.co.uk   Go   Links »

| Home | Destinations ▾ | Forum | Shop | Hotels & Hostels | Travel services |

Asia ▾ / India ▾

India
Practical information

INDIA
Overview
Places in India
When to go & weather
Getting there & around
Practical information
  Money & costs
  Health & safety
  Visas
Work & study

Money

The Indian rupee (Rs) is divided into 100 paise (p). Coins come in <u>denominations</u> of 5, 10, 20, 25 and 50 paise, and Rs 1, 2 and 5; notes come in Rs 10, 20, 50, 100, 500 and 1,000. The Indian rupee is linked to a number of currencies, and its value is generally stable.

Remember, you must present your passport whenever you change currency or traveller's cheques.

ATMs

Modern 24-hour ATMs (cash machines) are found in most large towns and cities. Away from major towns, always carry cash or traveller's cheques as <u>backup</u>.

Always keep the emergency lost-and-stolen numbers for your credit cards in a safe place, separate from your cards, and report any loss or theft immediately.

Cash

Major currencies, such as US dollars, UK pounds and euros, are easy to change throughout India. A few banks also accept Australian, New Zealand and Canadian dollars, and Swiss francs. Private money changers accept a wider range of currencies.

Nobody in India ever seems to have change, so it's a good idea to <u>maintain</u> a stock of smaller currency: Rs 10, 20 and 50 notes.

You cannot take rupees out of India. However, you can change any <u>leftover</u> rupees back into foreign currency, most easily at the airport. Note that some airport banks will only change a minimum of Rs 1,000. You may require encashment certificates or a credit-card receipt, and you may also have to show your passport and airline ticket.

Credit cards

Credit cards are accepted at many shops, restaurants and hotels, and you can also use them to pay for flights and train tickets. Cash advances on major credit cards are also possible at some banks without ATMs. MasterCard and Visa are the most widely accepted cards.

International transfers

If you run out of money, someone at home can <u>wire</u> you money via money changers affiliated with Moneygram or Western Union.

Money changers

Private money changers are usually open for longer hours than banks, and they are found almost everywhere (many also double as internet cafés and travel agents). Some upmarket hotels may also change money, usually at well below the bank rate.

Traveller's cheques

All major brands are accepted in India, but some banks may only accept cheques from Amex and Thomas Cook. Pounds sterling and US dollars are the safest currencies, especially in smaller towns.

If you lose your cheques, contact the Amex or Thomas Cook office in Delhi. To replace lost traveller's cheques, you need the <u>proof-of-purchase slip</u> and the numbers of the missing cheques (some places require a photocopy of the police report and a passport photo).

1 Before you watch, think about this question: how do you manage your money? Tick (✓) the things you do.

1 carry cash with you ☐ _AL_
2 use a credit card ☐ _____
3 use internet banking ☐ _____
4 check your bank account online ☐ _____
5 go into a branch of your bank ☐ _____
6 send money by mobile phone ☐ _____
7 ring your bank to check your account ☐ _____
8 go into a shop to send money to someone ☐ _____

2 Watch the video. Who talks about doing the things in Exercise 1? Write AL (Anna Laura) or M (Mainda).

Anna Laura

Mainda

3 Are the sentences true or false? Watch the video again to help you.

1 Anna Laura thinks cash is better than credit cards when travelling. TRUE / FALSE
2 Anna Laura thinks it's easier to check her account online than to go to a bank. TRUE / FALSE
3 Anna Laura's father has started to use online banking. TRUE / FALSE
4 Mainda says there have been big changes in mobile phone technology in recent years. TRUE / FALSE
5 Mainda thinks sending money by mobile is not a good use of technology. TRUE / FALSE

4 Anna Laura talks about her father's problems with online banking. Circle the correct verb forms to complete the extract, then watch again (00:11–01:13) to check.

My father, who is 82, ¹(has recently discovered) / is recently discovering how wonderful it is to use internet banking, but the problem with him, because he's 82, ²he's only learning / he's only learned very recently how to use a computer, and so when ³he's done / he's doing his internet banking things, ⁴he gets / he's getting stuck and ⁵picks up / picked up the phone to me.

5 Which is the correct description of how to send money by phone, according to Mainda?

1 You pay money in a shop and send a text message to another person. That person uses the message to collect the money from another shop.
2 You pay money in a shop. The shop sends the money to another shop, which sends a text message to the other person to collect the money.

6 Have you ever sent money to someone in another town or country? How did you do it?

GLOSSARY

wherever you are, wherever I am: in any place or situation
branch (noun): one of the offices of a bank or company
state (noun): the condition or situation of something at the moment
get stuck (verb): If you **get stuck** when you are doing something, you can't go on because it's difficult or you have a problem.
for instance: for example
user (noun): a person who uses a service or a product

6 Energy

VOCABULARY

Household chores

1 Complete the advice on this website about household chores.

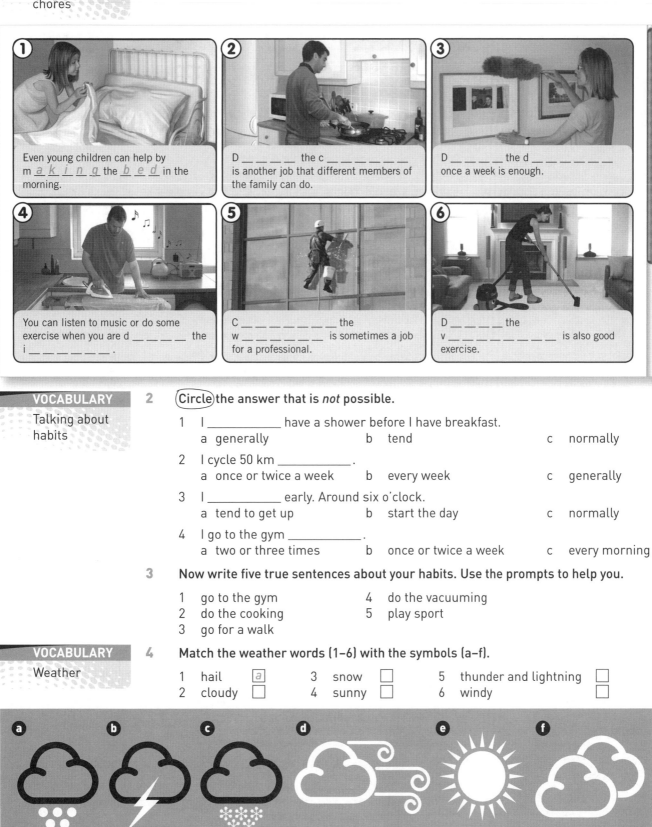

1 Even young children can help by m _a k i n g_ the _b e d_ in the morning.

2 D _ _ _ _ _ _ the c _ _ _ _ _ _ _ _ is another job that different members of the family can do.

3 D _ _ _ _ _ _ the d _ _ _ _ _ _ _ _ once a week is enough.

4 You can listen to music or do some exercise when you are d _ _ _ _ _ _ the i _ _ _ _ _ _ _ _ .

5 C _ _ _ _ _ _ _ _ _ _ the w _ _ _ _ _ _ _ _ _ is sometimes a job for a professional.

6 D _ _ _ _ _ _ the v _ _ _ _ _ _ _ _ _ _ is also good exercise.

VOCABULARY

Talking about habits

2 Circle the answer that is *not* possible.

1 I _____ have a shower before I have breakfast.
   a generally   b tend   c normally

2 I cycle 50 km _____ .
   a once or twice a week   b every week   c generally

3 I _____ early. Around six o'clock.
   a tend to get up   b start the day   c normally

4 I go to the gym _____ .
   a two or three times   b once or twice a week   c every morning

3 Now write five true sentences about your habits. Use the prompts to help you.

1 go to the gym   4 do the vacuuming
2 do the cooking   5 play sport
3 go for a walk

VOCABULARY

Weather

4 Match the weather words (1–6) with the symbols (a–f).

1 hail   `a`   3 snow   ☐   5 thunder and lightning   ☐
2 cloudy ☐   4 sunny   ☐   6 windy   ☐

a   b   c   d   e   f

5 Match the different kinds of weather in the box to the explanations (1–6).

A rainbow   Hail   Heavy rain   Lightning   ~~Thunder~~   Tornado

---

www.wheredoesweathercomefrom.com

1 _Thunder_

The lightning makes the air around it very, very hot – up to 33,000°C. As this air gets cooler, it makes a shock wave, and this is the loud sound that we hear. The closer the lightning is, the louder the noise we hear.

2 _____

Large electrical fields build up in the clouds. When they become very large, they 'spark', and this causes the flash of light that we see, as the electrical energy travels between the clouds and the ground.

3 _____

Sometimes in a thunderstorm, warm, wet air meets hot, dry air, and the wind makes it spin in a circle. The warm, wet air is pulled upwards and makes a giant column of air. They can reach speeds of up to 480kph.

4 _____

Warm air rises and forms drops of water. These drops join together in clouds. When the drops get big enough and get heavier, they fall from the sky.

5 _____

Strong winds lift rain high into the sky where it freezes and becomes ice. The ice is heavy, so it falls to the ground.

6 _____

When sunlight meets water in the air, the light is split into its different colours. The physics is complicated, but from the ground it looks like the light is 'bent' to make an arch.

GRAMMAR
Comparing things

6 (Circle) the correct form of the adjectives.

1 Sydney is the big / bigger / (biggest) city in Australia.
2 In Australia, December is usually hot / hotter / hottest than August.
3 The Sydney Festival is the important / more important / most important arts festival in Australia.
4 Melbourne is far / further / furthest south than Sydney.
5 The Opera House is a beautiful / more beautiful / most beautiful building.
6 Rugby League is the popular / more popular / most popular sport in Sydney.

7 Complete the paragraph about Hong Kong with the adjectives from the box in the correct form.

cloudy   cool   ~~good~~   hot   wet

Over to you

Write some sentences about the weather in your country.
What is the hottest time of year?
When is the best time of year to visit?
When is it wettest?

The [1] _best_ months to visit Hong Kong are November and December. The temperature then is [2] _____ than it is in summer, and it is usually dry, too. January and February are also cool, but you might not see so much sun because it is [3] _____ than November and December.
May to August is the [4] _____ part of the year, with temperatures of over 30°C. August is also the [5] _____ month of the year, with 390mm of rain, on average.

MYEnglish

8 Sandra is learning English in London. Read her self-assessment form.
Which things does Sandra find difficult?

1 Talking about habits   3 Speaking politely
2 Talking about the weather   4 Prepositions

Sandra, Sweden

SELF-ASSESSMENT

Can you do these things in English? Circle a number on each line.
1 = I can't do this, 5 = I can do this well.

⊚ talk about present habits	1 2 3 4 ⑤
⊚ talk about weather	1 2 3 4 ⑤
⊚ make comparisons	1 2 3 ④ 5
⊚ express preferences	1 2 3 ④ 5
⊚ speak more politely by being less direct	1 2 ③ 4 5

Comments

Talking about the weather! I didn't think it was true, but people really do talk a lot about the weather here. It's a very important thing to learn!

I think I can do most of these things well apart from the last one. I think it's difficult to get the right level of politeness in English. Swedish feels much more direct than English. I worry that if I try to translate from Swedish into English, I will be too direct and people might be upset or think that I am rude. People here say 'to be honest' a lot. It makes me think they aren't honest when they don't say it!

(And another thing – it isn't on the form, but I still have a big problem with prepositions! I still translate from Swedish and say 'in' too much. I need to learn my prepositions!)

Your English

9 What about you? Do you think it is difficult to speak more politely in English?
Do you think it is *important* to be polite in English?

10 Make these sentences less direct (and therefore more polite). Use some of the expressions from the box to help you.

really   Would you mind -ing?   Do you think you could … ?   Could you … ?   please   not very

1 Wait here. *Would you mind waiting here? / Could you wait here, please?*
2 I don't like football. _____
3 Be quiet. _____
4 This is boring. _____
5 What time is it? _____

11 Sandra also said she had a problem with prepositions. Are prepositions in your language different from English prepositions?

12 Complete the sentences using the prepositions in the box.

at for in ~~in~~ on

1 What's the weather like __*in*__ your country?
2 Manuel bought a treadmill and put it _____ the corner of his office.
3 He got better _____ working while he walked.
4 Alex cycles _____ 45 minutes to wash and dry his clothes.
5 The fastest winds _____ Earth are inside a tornado.

EXPLOREWriting

13 Read the hotel reviews from a review web page and answer this question: Who liked the Silver Bear Hotel, Peter H or Matt C?

File   Edit   View   Favorites   Tools   Help

Address   www.hotelreviewer.com/oslo/silverbearhotel   Go   Links »

Silver Bear Hotel, Oslo
★★★

Peter H from Lisbon **recommends** *this hotel.*
I was very pleased with this beautiful hotel. The room was big, and the bathroom was great. Also, I think it's the cleanest hotel I have ever stayed in. The staff were friendlier than in other hotels I have visited in Oslo. They were always ready to help.
The hotel is a little far from the city centre, but it's in a quiet area and it was easy to get to the centre by public transport. I'd rather have a comfortable hotel at a good price than be right in the city centre.
Just one complaint – the breakfast could have been better, but apart from that I would definitely recommend this hotel.

Matt C from London **does not recommend** *this hotel.*
A very disappointing stay. The room was big, but the bathroom wasn't very clean, and the towels were too small – the bed was uncomfortable, too.
I prefer to stay near the city centre, and this hotel is too far from there – a long tram ride.
The hotel staff were rude and unhelpful, and as well as that, this has to be the worst place in the city to change money.
I have stayed in Oslo several times, and this is the worst hotel I've stayed in in the city. I won't be going back.

---

14 Write the adjectives and adjectival phrases in the correct column of the table.

~~big~~   comfortable   could have been better   disappointing   far from the centre
friendly   great   in a quiet area   not very clean   ready to help   rude   too small
uncomfortable   unhelpful

positive	negative
big	

15 Complete the sentences from another hotel review using the expressions in the box.

could have been cleaner   don't mind   more expensive   ~~The best~~   would prefer

1   Very good. _The best_ hotel I have ever stayed in.

2   The room was OK, but it _____ . The windows in our room were very dirty.

3   I _____ to stay somewhere nearer the centre.

4   The hotel is OK if you _____ the noise of the motorway outside.

5   It is _____ than other hotels in the city.

16 Match the indirect / more polite sentences (1–5) with their more direct meaning (a–e).

1   It could be cheaper.   a   It took an hour by bus.
2   It wasn't very close to the city centre.   b   It tasted horrible.
3   The bed could have been more comfortable.   c   It's very expensive.
4   The food wasn't very good.   d   It was impossible to sleep.
5   The room was a bit small.   e   It was *very* small!

17 Write a review for the web page of a hotel you have stayed in. It can be a good review or a bad review. If you can't think of a hotel, invent one. Think about: the rooms, the staff, the location.

1 Before you watch, think about this question: what's your favourite season?
What's the weather like at that time of year?

Freda

Anna

Laura

2 Watch the video and match the topics (a–c) with the speakers (1–3).

a the different climates in one country
b a very cold holiday
c the differences between summer and winter

3 Watch again. Are the sentences true or false?

1 People in Finland talk more in winter.	TRUE / FALSE
2 In Finland, people stay at home more in summer.	TRUE / FALSE
3 Anna likes the climate in Australia.	TRUE / FALSE
4 The coldest parts of Australia are in the mountains and in the south.	TRUE / FALSE
5 Laura left Rio de Janeiro in winter.	TRUE / FALSE
6 Laura and her friends had the wrong clothes for Tierra del Fuego.	TRUE / FALSE

4 Watch Freda again (00:11–00:50). Complete the sentences using *quite* or *really*.

1 The summer in Finland is _____ warm, and the days are _____ , _____ long. In the winter, it's cold and it's dark, and the days are _____ short. And people are _____ different in the summer.

2 In the winter, people tend to be just _____ shy and they don't speak as much to each other.

5 Watch Anna again (00:55–01:46). (Circle) the correct word to complete these sentences.

1 Anna really / quite likes Australia.
2 The climate is really / quite hot inland, close to the desert.
3 When you get closer to the Antarctic, the climate gets really / quite cold.
4 Anna thinks there's really / quite a lot of choice of different climates in Australia.

6 Watch Laura again (01:51–02:27). Write *really* (x3) and *quite* (x1) in the correct places to complete this summary of her story.

really
It was /\ hot when they left Rio de Janeiro, but when they got to Tierra del Fuego, it was cold. They didn't have the right clothes, but they wrapped up warm with all the clothes they had. They stayed indoors a lot, but they did go out and see some penguins.

7 What's the climate like in your country? Is it very different in different parts of the country?

GLOSSARY

the tropics (plural noun): the band of the earth immediately north and south of the equator
inland (adjective): away from the sea
the height of summer: the middle of summer, the hottest part of summer
resort to (verb): If you **resort to** something, you do something you wouldn't usually do – perhaps because you have no choice.

7 City life

1 Complete what the people say about environmental problems using the words in the box.

> climate   flooding   ~~gas~~   oil   polluted   sea level   traffic   transport

1 It's really important that we use more energy from sun and wind, and less from ____*gas*____ and _____ .

2 We had really heavy rain and a lot of _____ in our area last year.

3 The air here is really _____ ; there are just too many cars.

4 Now petrol is so expensive, maybe there'll be less _____ on the roads.

5 I live on the coast, and the _____ is rising every year.

6 I know _____ change is a serious problem, but for us it's nice to have warmer summers!

7 We need to develop more efficient forms of _____ for the future.

2 Look at the statements in Exercise 1 again.

1 Which person quite likes the result of climate change?
2 Which two people describe problems related to water?
3 Which two people describe changes we need to make?
4 Which person hopes to see a positive result from a problem?

3 Match the sentences (1–3) with the definitions (a–c).

1 The traffic in the city will get worse.
2 There won't be more flooding in the future.
3 The sea might (not) become more polluted.

a I'm sure this will happen.
b It's possible that this will happen.
c There's no chance that this will happen.

4 What do you think city life will be like in 2050? Complete the sentences with *will*, *won't*, *might* or *may* to give your opinion.

1 People _____ leave big cities; they _____ live in smaller towns.
2 City transport _____ be very different from today.
3 Rich people _____ live in the city centres.
4 Buildings _____ become taller.
5 Old historic cities _____ be destroyed to build more efficient towns.
6 It _____ become less expensive to live in a city.
7 Schools and universities _____ be on campuses outside the cities.
8 Green space and parks _____ be used for building houses.
9 It _____ be more difficult to find work in the cities.
10 People _____ stay at home more in their free time.

Over to you

What other changes do you think there will be in city life in the future? Write a sentence or record yourself speaking on the DVD-ROM.

GRAMMAR

Real conditionals

5 **Match the two parts of the sentences.**

1 If you leave now,
2 If you like Italian food,
3 If you go there in spring,
4 If you buy a smaller car,
5 If you like world music,
6 If you write to the company,

a you should listen to this band.
b they might send you some information.
c you'll see the trees full of flowers.
d you'll pay less for petrol.
e you should go to Pizza Plus.
f you might get the five o'clock train.

6 **Circle the correct verb forms to complete the sentences.**

1 Daniel helps / will help her tomorrow if she has / she'll have any problems.
2 If you go / you'll go to the end of the road, you see / you'll see a cinema on your left.
3 I send / I'll send you the photo if I find / I'll find it.
4 If I have / I might have time, I call / I might call them.
5 If you go / you should go to New York, you go / you should go to Central Park.
6 If you look / you'll look on my desk, you see / you'll see a black diary.

VOCABULARY

Giving directions

7 **Look at the map of the city centre and follow the directions a local person gives the tourist at the train station. Find the tourist office on the map: a, b, c or d.**

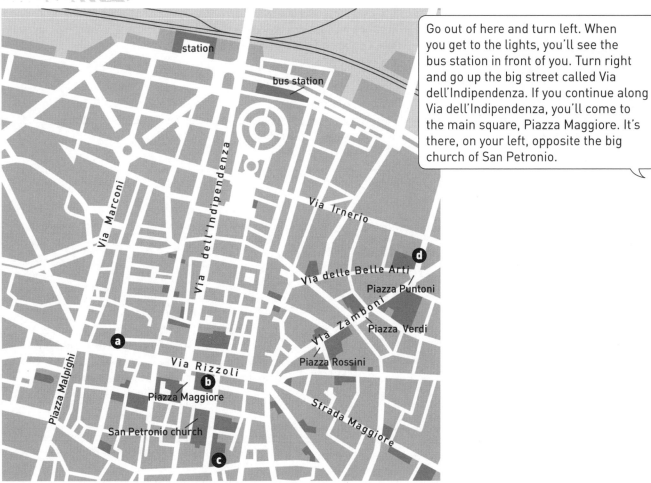

Go out of here and turn left. When you get to the lights, you'll see the bus station in front of you. Turn right and go up the big street called Via dell'Indipendenza. If you continue along Via dell'Indipendenza, you'll come to the main square, Piazza Maggiore. It's there, on your left, opposite the big church of San Petronio.

8 **Complete the directions from the tourist office to the art gallery using the phrases in the box.**

| Go along   go past   on your   out of   turn   you continue   you'll come   you'll see |

Go ¹ _out of_ here and go back to Via Rizzoli. Turn right and ² _____ two big towers in front of you. ³ _____ Via Rizzoli, and when you come to the towers, ⁴ _____ left down Via Zamboni. If ⁵ _____ down this road, you'll ⁶ _____ two small squares ⁷ _____ right, then ⁸ _____ to another little square, called Piazza Puntoni. The gallery is on the corner of that square, in Via delle Belle Arti.

Getting tourist information

9 Cross out the word that does *not* go with each bold phrase.

1 **I'm looking for** a bed and breakfast / ~~day trips~~ / somewhere to stay.
2 **Do you organise** city tours / trips / a map ?
3 **Have you got** a map / a restaurant / any leaflets ?
4 **Can you recommend** somewhere to eat / a good hotel / leaflets ?
5 **Do you have any information about** the bus station / museums / things to do ?
6 **Do you sell** guidebooks / travel passes / art galleries ?

10 Complete the tourist's questions in the tourist office. Use the expressions in bold from Exercise 9.

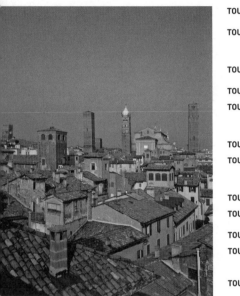

TOURIST OFFICER Hello, can I help you?

TOURIST Yes, I've just arrived, and ¹ *I'm looking for* the bed and breakfast I booked online. ²_____ a map?

TOURIST OFFICER Yes, here you are. We're here, in the main square.

TOURIST OK, thanks. And ³_____ the museums or other things to see?

TOURIST OFFICER Right, here's a leaflet about all the museums and galleries, but it's a nice city just to walk around.

TOURIST ⁴_____ any city tours?

TOURIST OFFICER There's a walking tour in English tomorrow morning at 11 o'clock, starting from here. Or there's a bus tour that goes all day.

TOURIST ⁵_____ tickets for that?

TOURIST OFFICER No, you can just pay the bus driver.

TOURIST Great. One last question – ⁶_____ a cheap restaurant near here?

TOURIST OFFICER There's a pizzeria just across the square, or you'll find lots of cafés and fast-food places all along this road here.

TOURIST OK. Thanks very much.

TimeOut

11 Complete the crossword. All the answers are places in a city.

3 across: G A L L E R Y

ACROSS
3 It's a place where you go to see pictures or other works of art.
7 If you travel by train, you'll arrive here.
8 It's an open area in a city, with buildings around it.
9 This is a good way to visit a new place.
10 This is a waterway (in cities like Amsterdam and Venice).

DOWN
1 You can go here to get information about a city. (2 words)
2 This is another word for a park.
4 It's a place where you can see a collection of interesting things.
5 It's a big house where a royal or important family lives.
6 These are the interesting things you can see in a city or country.

EXPLORE**Reading**

12 Look at the web page about a short holiday in Cork, Ireland. Match the headings (1–9) with the information the sections contain (a–i).

1	Why go now?	a	a trip out of town
2	Touch down	b	a good time to visit
3	Check in	c	museums and galleries
4	Take a hike	d	somewhere to have a drink
5	Cultural afternoon	e	arriving at the airport
6	Window shopping	f	looking around the shops
7	An aperitif	g	somewhere to stay
8	Dining with the locals	h	a sightseeing walk
9	Take a ride	i	dinner in a restaurant

13 Read the information. Are these sentences true or false?

1 It's dark in summer before 9 p.m.   TRUE / FALSE
2 The only transport from the airport is by taxi. TRUE / FALSE
3 There is only one hostel in Cork.   TRUE / FALSE
4 Grand Parade was a canal before it was a street. TRUE / FALSE
5 Butter was important in Cork's history.   TRUE / FALSE
6 It's difficult to find traditional Irish pubs. TRUE / FALSE
7 Blarney Castle is in the centre of Cork.   TRUE / FALSE

Over to you

Do you think you would enjoy 48 hours in Cork? Write two sentences saying what you would do there.

14 According to the article, who would enjoy 48 hours in Cork?

1 people who enjoy walking in the countryside
2 only people who are interested in food and drink
3 people who like sightseeing and culture
4 young people who like clubbing

---

http://www.independenttravel/48-hours-in/cork.html

Home > Travel > 48 Hours In

Cork

▽ SHARE | ▤ PRINT ARTICLE | ✉ EMAIL ARTICLE | ᴬᴬ TEXT SIZE

by Simon Calder

Click here for 48 hours in ... Cork map

Why go now?

Ireland's second city is an ideal summer destination: friendly, compact, lively – and far enough west for the evening light in August to continue past 9 p.m.

Touch down

Non-stop flights operate to Cork from a wide range of British airports. Cork airport is five miles south of the centre. Two bus operators offer links to the city. A cab to the city centre costs €15–€20 (£12.50–£17).

Check in

MacCurtain Street has a range of accommodation – including the characterful three-star Hotel Isaacs at number 48. On the south side of town, Jurys is a stylish 21st-century hotel off Western Road. There are also plenty of B&Bs along Western Road. Cork has several backpacker hostels, of which the most attractive is Kinlay House on Bob & Joan's Walk.

Take a hike

Start at the National Monument just opposite the tourist office. Walk north, away from the river, along the handsome Grand Parade, which was once a waterway. Turn right into St Patrick's Street. Look to the left to see the Huguenot Quarter. Many Protestants from France came here in the 17th century, and it is now full of bars, restaurants and shops. At the north channel of the River Lee, turn right to follow Merchant's Quay, before walking south along Parnell Place. At the south channel, look across to the handsome City Hall.

Cultural afternoon

The Crawford Municipal Art Gallery on Emmet Place has been extended to show a wide range of Irish art. The Butter Museum in O'Connell Square explores butter's role in the development of Cork.

Window shopping

While St Patrick's Street is the main shopping area, Cornmarket Street is more interesting. It has the Coal Quay market and a new shopping mall, the Cornmarket Centre.

An aperitif

Most visitors are keen to find a traditional Irish pub. Happily, there are still many of these – such as Dennehy's on Cornmarket Street.

Dining with the locals

Gourmet vegetarian dishes are on the menu at Café Paradiso, at 16 Lancaster Quay. Scoozi's, at 314 Winthrop Avenue, is cheaper, meatier and more relaxed, and offers alfresco dining in summer.

Take a ride

Bus 224 departs from Merchant's Quay, taking 20 minutes to reach Blarney, which is five miles north-west. Blarney Castle is a 15th-century fortress residence in landscaped grounds. The climb to the tower is narrow and difficult, but the views are spectacular.

Interesting? Click here to explore further.

1 Before you watch, think about this quesion: which do you prefer, the city or the countryside?

2 Watch the video. Who talks about these things? Write J (Joanna) or L (Luis).

1 the place where he/she lives _____

2 a place where he/she goes on holiday _____

Joanna

3 According to Joanna, are the sentences true or false? Watch again (00:11–00:59) to check.

1 Gdansk is a city on the north coast of Poland.   TRUE / FALSE
2 Gdansk is a very long way from Sweden.   TRUE / FALSE
3 The north part of Sweden is very natural and wild.   TRUE / FALSE

4 According to Luis, are the sentences true or false? Watch again (01:05–01:45) to check.

1 Coffee is Colombia's biggest industry.   TRUE / FALSE
2 Colombia has a lot of natural resources.   TRUE / FALSE
3 Many Colombians have moved away from the cities.   TRUE / FALSE

Luis

5 Watch again (00:11–00:59) and try to complete what Joanna says using the adjectives in the box.

| appealing   intriguing   mysterious   unspoilt |

I particularly like its northern part, which is known as Europe's last wilderness, which means one of the few places that are ^{1}_____ and very ^{2}_____ . It will probably sound a little bit selfish, but I'm concerned that as more and more people discover this place for their own, it will become less ^{3}_____ and therefore, to me, less ^{4}_____ .

6 If you *spoil* something, you damage or destroy it. If something is a *mystery*, it is strange or difficult to understand. What do you think *unspoilt*, *mysterious* countryside is like?

7 Circle the correct meaning for these words.

1 *Intriguing* means fascinating / boring.
2 *Appealing* means large / attractive.

8 Complete the information about Colombia using the words in the box. Watch Luis again (01:05–01:45) to check.

| clothing   coat   coffee   financial   oil   printing |

COLOMBIA

Natural resources: ^{1}____coal____ , ^{2}_____
Agriculture: ^{3}_____
Business: ^{4}_____ services
Manufacturing: ^{5}_____ , ^{6}

9 Do you prefer to spend your free time in a very quiet place, or somewhere with a lot to see and do?

GLOSSARY

drawn to (verb): If you are **drawn to** something, you like it and find it interesting.
wilderness /ˈwɪldənəs/ (noun): a very wild area of land, with no buildings or agriculture
selfish (adjective): When you are **selfish**, you think about you, not about other people.
discover (verb): to find or learn about something
therefore (conjunction): so, as a result
coal (noun): a hard black mineral which you burn for heat
printing (noun): the production of newspapers, books, etc.
manufacturing (noun): making things in an industrial way

Unit 1

1 b calypso c salsa d hip-hop e reggae f classical music
g folk music

2 2 brought up; play 3 traditional 4 how 5 to

3 2 e 3 g 4 f 5 c

4 2 have a look 3 Hang on 4 think about 5 not really into
6 that looks 7 sounds 8 see if 9 idea

5 2 skiing 3 yoga 4 volleyball 5 hockey 6 karate
7 aerobics 8 swimming

6 1 karate 2 skiing 3 boxing

7 1 In heavy industrial sites and petro-chemical plants.
2 He's a singer.

8 Songs from the 1940s and '50s (and musicals).

9 2 Did; have 3 did; decide 4 does; sing
5 does; sing 6 Does; sing 7 is; doing

10 1 (He learned) by watching the films they were in again and again.
2 No, he had a terrible voice.
3 Because he wanted to join a musical group.
4 (He sings) in musicals.
5 (He usually sings) with the local (music) group.
6 Yes, he does.
7 He's preparing a part for the musical *Hello, Dolly!*.

11 1 True. Two teams of six players try to push a heavy circular
'puck' into a goal at the bottom of a swimming pool.
2 True. It's very popular in New Zealand, where it started.
3 False. They throw plastic discs, like Frisbees.
4 True. The players play chess for four minutes, then box for two
minutes, for up to 11 rounds.
5 True. Korfball is similar to basketball, and *korf* is the name for
the basket.

13 b 6 c 5 d 1 e 4 f 3

14 2 False 3 True 4 False

15 2 b 3 a 4 a 5 a 6 b

DVD-ROM Extra

2 1 b 2 c 3 a

3 1 H, C 2 M, C

4 3, 5, 4, 1, 2

5 2 black 3 white 4 19/nineteen 5 19/nineteen 6 larger

6 1 T 2 T 3 F (He liked football and basketball.)
4 F (He liked the people and the place.) 5 T

Unit 2

1 2 degree 3 exams 4 an exam 5 a degree 6 college
7 an exam 8 studies

2 2 It's the most difficult subject I've / I have ever studied.
3 I've / I have always enjoyed studying alone.
4 I've / I have done a lot of exams in my life.
5 I've / I have never written an essay in English.
6 I've / I have done several part-time courses.
7 She's the best teacher I've / I have ever had.
8 I've / I have never failed an exam.

3 2 holiday 3 pay 4 stressful 5 place 6 flexible
7 atmosphere 8 management 9 easy
10 part-time 11 at home

4 2 've/have known; since
3 's/has been; for
4 's/has worked; for
5 've/have lived; since
6 've/have liked; since
7 's/has played; since
8 's/has been; for

5 2 in 3 in 4 in 5 in 6 – 7 at 8 to

6 1 False 2 False 3 False

8 1 True 2 False

9 2 I would like
3 advertised
4 I have worked
5 I have studied
6 I enjoy
7 I have difficulty in
8 improve my spoken English
9 project the company's image effectively
10 Regards

DVD-ROM Extra

2 1 b 2 c

3 1 c 2 e 3 a 4 b 5 d

4 1 T 2 F (There was space for about 20 people.)
3 F (They didn't need a partner.) 4 T 5 T

5 2 back 3 really 4 so much 5 people

Unit 3

1 empty, friendly, convenient, expensive, noisy

2 2 modern/old-fashioned 3 cheap/expensive
4 inconvenient/convenient 5 quiet/noisy 6 crowded/empty

3 2 noisy 3 friendly 4 cheap 5 convenient

4 Waiter: 1, 2, 3, 5, 9, 11
Customer: 4, 6, 7, 8, 10, 12

5 2 No problem, come this way, please.
3 Are you ready to order?
4 And for you?
5 Me too, please – soup.
6 Anything to drink?
7 Could we have a bottle of water, please?
8 Sparkling or still?
9 Can we have the bill, please?

6 2 bottle of red wine 3 table in the corner
4 chicken in garlic sauce 5 meal for 25 people
6 menu with lots of vegetarian dishes

7 2 What about 3 How about 4 What about 5 How about
6 What should

9 2 chicken 3 mushrooms 4 prawns 5 pear 6 soup
7 pasta 8 cheese 9 strawberries 10 potatoes

10 1 b 2 c 3 a 4 d

11 1 c 2 b 3 d 4 a

12 Pete: Bella Napoli
Ravi: El Buho Azul
Sonia: The Taj

DVD-ROM Extra

2 almonds, anchovies, chicken, chilli, coconut rice, ginger,
monkey nuts, onions, pistachios, spring onions

3 1 lokum 2 nasi lemak 3 nasi lemak 4 lokum

4 1 had 2 became 3 opened

5 1 is 2 come 3 cook

6 Nilgun uses the past simple because she is relating facts from
the past.
Alex uses the present simple because he is describing facts that
are still true.

Unit 4

1 2 passengers 3 meter 4 fare 5 change 6 tip 7 receipt

2 2 T 3 P 4 T 5 P 6 P 7 T 8 P

3 1 How much is it to the airport?
2 Can I put my bags in the back?
3 Can you take me to Terminal 2, please?
4 That's $27.80, please.
5 can I have a receipt, please?
6 Have a good trip, then.

4 2 After 3 then 4 During 5 When

5 2 paid 3 realised 4 was crying 5 saw 6 gave

6 2 to 3 in 4 in/to 5 – 6 for 7 with 8 for 9 to 10 in/–

7 b 4 c 2 d 5 e 1

8 1 b 2 c 3 a

9 2 because 3 to 4 for 5 because 6 because 7 for 8 to

11 b

12 a 4 b 3 c 1 d 2

DVD-ROM Extra

1 2 French 3 Japanese 4 Japanese 5 Afghanistan 6 India

3 1 Switzerland 2 Swiss; Japanese 3 Afghan
4 English; French 5 English; French 6 India; Afghanistan
7 Hindi

4 1 magnificent; beautiful 2 nice 3 unusual 4 little
5 beautiful

5 2 family 3 different 4 actually 5 lifestyle

Unit 5

1 A 4 B 2 C 3

2 3 Sorry, do you have any smaller notes?
1 Hello. Can I change these euros into Canadian dollars, please?
4 Sure. Are twenties OK?
2 Of course. That's 50, 100, 150, 200 euros. So that's $332.22. Here you are.
5 Fine. Thanks.

3 2 pay 3 cards 4 PIN 5 receipt

4 1 How would you like to pay?
2 how much is it?
3 I'll pay in cash.
4 Do you have anything smaller?

5 2 d 3 a 4 e 5 c

6 2 can 3 don't have to 4 should 5 Don't 6 shouldn't
7 shouldn't 8 don't have to 9 shouldn't 10 You have to

7 Across: 4 currency 5 cash 6 coins 7 PIN 8 notes
Down: 1 dollars 2 by 3 receipt 4 change

8 All of them

9 2 Bad 3 Bad 4 Good 5 Bad 6 Good 7 Bad 8 Good

10 2 b 3 a 4 a 5 b 6 b

DVD-ROM Extra

2 2 AL 3 AL 4 AL 5 AL 6 M 7 AL 8 M

3 1 F (She thinks credit cards are better.) 2 T 3 T 4 T
5 F (She thinks it is a good use of technology.)

4 2 he's only learned 3 he's doing 4 he gets 5 picks up

5 1

Unit 6

1 2 Doing [the] cooking
3 Doing [the] dusting
4 doing [the] ironing
5 Cleaning [the] windows
6 Doing [the] vacuuming

2 1 b 2 c 3 c 4 a

4 2 f 3 c 4 e 5 b 6 d

5 2 Lightning 3 Tornado 4 Heavy rain 5 Hail 6 A rainbow

6 2 hotter 3 most important 4 further 5 beautiful
6 most popular

7 2 cooler 3 cloudier 4 hottest 5 wettest

8 3 and 4

10 Example answers
2 I don't **really** like football.
3 **Could you** be quiet, **please?** / **Would you mind being** quiet, **please?** / **Do you think you could** be quiet, **please?**
4 This **isn't very interesting**.
5 **Could you tell me** the time, **please?**

12 2 in 3 at 4 for 5 on

13 Peter H

14

positive	negative
big	could have been better
comfortable	disappointing
friendly	far from the centre
great	not very clean
in a quiet area	rude
ready to help	too small
	uncomfortable
	unhelpful

15 2 could have been cleaner 3 would prefer 4 don't mind
5 more expensive

16 2 a 3 d 4 b 5 e

DVD-ROM Extra

2 1 c 2 a 3 b

3 1 F (They stay at home more in winter.)
2 F (They talk less in winter.) 3 T 4 T
5 F (They left Rio in summer.) 6 T

4 1 quite; really; really; really; really
2 quite

5 1 really 2 really 3 really 4 quite

6 It was **really** hot when they left Rio de Janeiro, but when they got to Tierra del Fuego, it was **really** cold. They didn't have the right clothes, but they wrapped up **really** warm with all the clothes they had. They stayed indoors **quite** a lot, but they did go out and see some penguins.

Unit 7

1 1 oil 2 flooding 3 polluted 4 traffic
5 sea level 6 climate 7 transport

2 1 6 2 2,5 3 1,7 4 4

3 1 a 2 c 3 b

5 2 e 3 c 4 d 5 a 6 b

6 1 she has 2 you go; you'll see 3 I'll send; I find
4 I have; I might call 5 you go; you should go
6 you look; you'll see

7 The tourist office is b.

8 2 you'll see 3 Go along 4 turn 5 you continue 6 go past
7 on your 8 you'll come

9 2 a map 3 a restaurant 4 leaflets 5 the bus station
6 art galleries

10 2 Have you got
3 do you have any information about
4 Do you organise
5 Do you sell
6 can you recommend

11 Across: 7 station 8 square 9 tour 10 canal
Down: 1 tourist office 2 gardens 4 museum 5 palace
6 sights

12 2 e 3 g 4 h 5 c 6 f 7 d 8 i 9 a

13 2 False 3 False 4 True 5 True 6 False 7 False

14 people who like sightseeing and culture

DVD-ROM Extra

2 1 L 2 J

3 1 T 2 F (Gdansk is very close to Sweden.) 3 T

4 1 F (It's not the biggest business any more.) 2 T
3 F (They have moved away from the countryside.)

5 1 unspoilt 2 mysterious 3 intriguing 4 appealing

6 wild, unpolluted, without buildings, and with quite a strange atmosphere

7 1 fascinating 2 attractive

8 2 oil 3 coffee 4 financial 5 printing 6 clothing

Unit 8

1 2 b 3 h 4 c 5 g 6 j 7 e 8 i 9 a 10 d 11 f

2 2 What size is it?
3 Can I try it on?
4 Do you have any other colours?
5 How much do you want for it?
6 Would you take 25?
7 OK, I'll take it.
8 thanks, but I'll leave it.

3 2 U 3 U 4 U 5 U 6 C

4 2 any; colours 3 any; CDs 4 some rice; any meat
5 some information

5 2 weighs 3 made of 4 wood 5 with 6 light 7 dark

6 2 was designed 3 is/'s made of 4 Was it designed
5 was designed 6 was it made 7 was made

7 2 h 3 c 4 d 5 a 6 g 7 b 8 e

8 2 It's made of
3 I've had it since
4 It was given to me by
5 it reminds me of
6 I absolutely love it because
7 I need it for
8 helps me to

9 1 She wanted to buy a red T-shirt.
2 She stressed the wrong word in the sentence.

11 2 Jan's wearing the blue <u>T-shirt</u>.
3 Can I see the <u>smaller</u> one?
4 Carlos is sitting next to <u>Adam</u>.
5 Carlos is <u>sitting</u> next to Adam.

12 2 True 3 False (The seller is reluctant to sell the vase.) 4 True
5 False (The buyer pays postage.)

13 2 8.6cm tall and 5cm wide
3 approximately
4 dark
5 pattern
6 manufactured by
7 rare
8 collectable
9 reluctant
10 postage

14 2, 4, 5, 6, 7, 8, 10, 12

DVD-ROM Extra

2 1 c 2 a 3 b

3 2 AL 3 AL 4 J 5 L 6 AL 7 L

4 2 brings back 3 shape of 4 been in 5 allowed; to

Unit 9

1 2 e 3 h 4 b 5 g 6 c 7 a 8 d

2 2 angry 3 starving 4 freezing 5 terrified 6 tired/exhausted
7 amazed 8 boiling

3 2 You're welcome!
3 Don't mention it.
4 Well done.
5 I'm sorry to hear that.

4 2 f 3 d 4 b 5 c 6 a 7 h 8 i 9 e

5 2 's started 3 've found 4 's opened 5 've made 6 've had
7 've learned/learnt 8 've visited

6 1 what's new with you?
2 What have you been up to
3 How are James and the kids?
4 how are things at work?

7 1 True. Some scientists think this is evidence that dogs can understand human emotions.
2 False. It can help to 'pop' your ears and stop them hurting.
3 False. They usually try not to make eye contact.
4 False. Chimpanzees and other monkeys also smile when they are happy.
5 True.

6 True.
7 True. This is called 'photic sneeze reflex', and about 20–30% of people have this reaction.
8 False. Most people naturally close their eyes, but some people can keep them open.

8 1 False 2 True 3 True

9 1 red 2 open; an open 3 opens 4 quietly 5 easy
6 doesn't look; moves

10 2 c 3 d 4 e 5 f 6 b

DVD-ROM Extra

2 2 S/P 3 P 4 S 5 S

3 1 T 2 F (He didn't understand English or Mandarin.) 3 T
4 F (She drew a picture.)

4 2 which 3 why 4 what 5 how 6 where

5 1 was 2 used 3 thought 4 didn't use

6 2 surprised 3 had this image 4 fascinated 5 looking at
6 thinking; thought

Unit 10

1 2 restaurant 3 health club 4 laundry
5 wireless internet access

2 2 health club 3 restaurants 4 air conditioned
5 wireless internet 6 laundry service
7 business centre

3 2 G 3 G 4 G 5 R a G b R c G d R e R

4 2 d 3 b 4 e 5 a

6 2 are going / are going to go
3 are meeting / are going to meet
4 is going to be
5 is

8 2 make a mistake 3 make dinner
4 make a lot of money 5 make new friends
6 make arrangements

9 1, 3, 4, 5

14 1 b 2 c 3 a

15 1 She's staying
Pete, Kumiko and the kids are coming
You're staying
2 is going to drive
I'm going to make
she's going to bring
3 What time does your flight arrive?

DVD-ROM Extra

2 1 c 2 b

3 1 M 2 R 3 R 4 M

4 1 Internet; email; sites 2 share; share; emails 3 chatrooms
4 chatrooms; websites 5 blog

Unit 11

1 b 3 c 4 d 7 e 6 f 5 g 1 h 2

2 2 spacious 3 traditional 4 large 5 modern 6 cool
7 warm

3 2 bad 3 trouble 4 thing 5 good

5 2

6 2 should 3 'd 4 Would 5 'd

8 1 traditional 2 large 3 warm 4 spacious 5 fireplace
6 balcony 7 cool 8 parking 9 garden 10 barbecue
11 modern

9 Seven

10 2 two
3 two out of: full double glazing, the fireplace in the lounge, the radiators, the heated towel rail in the bathroom
4 the rear garden
5 the front garden

11 2 paved 3 lawn 4 hob 5 throughout 6 built-in
    7 double glazing 8 hand basin 9 fully fitted 10 tiled
12 1 The house doesn't have enough bedrooms.
    2 Cathryn might have problems going up and down the stairs.
    3 Craig and Marta want a house in a quiet location, but this house
      is near the city centre and railway station.

DVD-ROM Extra

2 1 S 2 V 3 V 4 S
3 1 d 2 a 3 b 4 c
4 The past simple
5 1 N 2 N 3 P 4 P 5 P
6 1 was; were 2 were 3 studied; became; learnt/learned
   4 hated; started 5 changed; became
7 The verbs are all in the past simple. We use the past simple to talk
   about experiences in the past that are now finished.

Unit 12

1 2 the north; borders 3 island; south-east of 4 between
   5 coast of 6 in; the east 7 coast 8 nation 9 west of
2 2 d 3 i 4 g 5 b 6 f 7 e 8 c 9 a
3 Europe: c, d Australasia: i Africa: e, f Asia: g, h
   South America: a North America: b
4 1 Europe 2 the Mediterranean
5 2 **The population is** about 400,000.
   3 **The official languages are** Maltese and English.
   4 **It's a member of** the EU, the British Commonwealth and the UN.
   5 It **makes its money from** manufacturing, services and tourism.
   6 In **the past**, it was ruled by the Greeks, Romans and Phoenicians.
   7 It **became independent** in 1964.
   8 It's **famous for** ancient temples and beautiful beaches.
6 2 a 3 g 4 f 5 b 6 h 7 d 8 c
7 2 to become 3 to study 4 to study 5 qualifying 6 leaving
   7 improving 8 to continue
8 2 You probably **know** that he fought in the Cuban revolution.
   3 I don't **know** much about his early life.
   4 I **know** that he was born in Argentina.
   5 I don't really **know** for sure, but I think he worked as a doctor.
   6 As far as I **know**, he spent most of his adult life in Cuba.
   7 I don't **know** when he died, but I **know** it was in Bolivia.
9 1 Spanish 2 Nigeria 3 Morocco (Arabic and French) 4 Italy
12 1 False 2 True
13 a 3,4 b 2 c 1 d 1,5
14 2 After 3 where 4 also 5 During 6 but

DVD-ROM Extra

2 2 I 3 MF 4 I/MF 5 MF
3 3, 4, 1, 2
4 b
5 1 very 2 not typical 3 hasn't
6 2 his 3 in 4 in 5 on

Unit 13

1 2 I think I would die without it.
   3 I couldn't live without it.
   4 I don't know how to use them.
   5 I need to have it with me.
   6 I don't even have one at home.
   7 I use it for my job.
   8 I use it all the time.
   9 I don't bother with it.
   10 It makes life easier.
2 a 2, 3, 5, 7, 8, 10
   b 1, 4, 6, 9

3 2 calling 3 It's 4 moment 5 here 6 take 7 call 8 that
   9 This 10 good 11 reception 12 back
4 2 Incorrect 3 Correct 4 Correct 5 Correct 6 Correct
5 1 would 2 used to; would 3 used to; would 4 used to; used to
   5 used to; would
6 In the **past**, I'd put all of my photos into a photo album. **These**
   days, I store all my photos in digital format online
   In the **days** before the Internet, I used to buy CDs. **Nowadays**,
   I download all of my music from iTunes.
   There are more opportunities for wasting time at work than **there**
   used to be. I do much less work than I **used** to!
9 a 3 b 6 c 9 d 1 e 5 f 8 g 2 h 7 i 4
10 1 b 2 b
11 2 insert/load 3 slide 4 raise 5 plug in 6 click

DVD-ROM Extra

2 1 M 2 M 3 M/I
3 2 a couple of 3 didn't understand 4 a kind of game
   5 doesn't know
4 1 b 2 d 3 a 4 c
5 1 wave 2 seal 3 flippers
6 used to
7 No. You can only use *would* with actions, not with state verbs like
   love, like, be, etc.

Unit 14

1 2 I **find** it quite exciting.
   3 We all **know** that people are aggressive.
   4 And **anyway**, nobody has to box.
   5 I really **feel** that if people want to box, we shouldn't stop them.
   6 Of **course** that's not the same.
   7 The thing **is**, they have rules and there's a referee.
   8 Another **thing** is, being a boxer is a job, you know.
2 2 D 3 D 4 F 5 A 6 A
4 2 won't fly 3 would/'d reduce 4 walked; drove
   5 would/'d reduce 6 wouldn't need 7 buy 8 will have to
5 2 P 3 I 4 I 5 I 6 I 7 P 8 P
6 1 A 2 D 3 N 4 A 5 N
7 b 3 c 2 d 1 e 5
9 *Example answer*
   3 People who disagree in a very direct way in English can
     sometimes sound rude.
10 b: write to the press
13 2 a 3 c 4 b 5 d 6 b 7 c 8 b

DVD-ROM Extra

2 Amanda: a Claire: b
3 1 T 2 T 3 F (They have different opinions.)
   4 F (She didn't like either dance or gymnastics.)
   5 F (She wanted to do a martial art when she was seven, but she
     didn't start until she was 14.) 6 T
4 2 e 3 a 4 b 5 c 6 f 7 g
5 1 have a debate; take decisions
   2 look after
   3 do a martial art
   4 do gymnastics
   5 disagreed with
   6 gave; a hard time

8 Things

1 Match the two parts of the sentences.

1	No, thanks. I'm just	a	is it?
2	Can I have	b	a look at that jacket?
3	Can I see	c	you a hundred.
4	I could give	d	on?
5	OK, I'll	e	leave it.
6	Would you take	f	have any other colours?
7	Thanks, but I'll	g	take it.
8	How much do you	h	the one at the top?
9	What size	i	want for it?
10	Can I try it	j	25?
11	Do you	k	looking.

2 Complete the conversation with sentences from Exercise 1. You will not need all of the sentences.

> **STALLHOLDER** Hello. Do you need any help?
>
> **CUSTOMER** Yes, ¹*can I have a look at that jacket* ? The red one with the green buttons.
>
> **STALLHOLDER** This one?
>
> **CUSTOMER** Yes, that's the one. ² _____ ?
>
> **STALLHOLDER** It's a large.
>
> **CUSTOMER** ³ _____ ?
>
> **STALLHOLDER** Yes, of course.
>
> **CUSTOMER** Mm. ⁴ _____ ?
>
> **STALLHOLDER** I'm afraid not, no. Only red.
>
> **CUSTOMER** OK. ⁵ _____ ?
>
> **STALLHOLDER** It's 35.
>
> **CUSTOMER** ⁶ _____ ?
>
> **STALLHOLDER** I can take 30.
>
> **CUSTOMER** ⁷ _____ . Can I pay by credit card?
>
> **STALLHOLDER** Sorry, cash only.
>
> **CUSTOMER** Oh, OK. Well, in that case ⁸ _____ .
>
> **STALLHOLDER** OK. Bye then.

3 Are these words countable or uncountable? Write *C* or *U*.

1 colour ☐C☐ 3 rice ☐ 5 information ☐
2 help ☐ 4 meat ☐ 6 CD ☐

4 Complete the sentences with the correct form of the words from Exercise 3 plus *some* or *any*.

1 **A** Are you OK there? Can I help with anything?
  B Actually, erm, I do need *some* *help* . Can you tell me where the milk is, please?
2 **A** Do you have this in _____ other _____ ?
  B Yes, I think we have it in green and blue. I'll just check.
3 **A** Excuse me?
  B Yes, hi.
  A Do you have _____ Mozart _____ ?
  B Sure. Just over here.
4 **A** I'll cook tonight.
  B Great. There's _____ _____ in the cupboard.
  A OK. And do you have _____ _____ ? Chicken or something?
  B I'll just look in the fridge.
5 **A** Hello, can you give me _____ _____ about the market?
  B Of course. Well, it's open from …

8

5 Complete the items for sale on this website using the words in the box.

~~by~~   dark   light   made of   weighs   with   wood

Rare 1970s Apple mirror. It's 36 ¹ _by_ 29.5 centimetres, and it ² _____ about 10 kilograms.

1960s coat rack, ³ _____ ⁴ _____ and metal.

1950s wardrobe ⁵ _____ two doors and six drawers. The large door is ⁶ _____ blue and the small one is ⁷ _____ blue.

6 Some customers call the shop in Exercise 5 to find out more information about the objects above. Complete the conversations with the passive form of the verbs in brackets.

CUSTOMER 1 Hi, I'm calling about an item that ¹ _is advertised_ (advertise) on your website – the Apple mirror.

SALES ASSISTANT Yes, I know the one. What would you like to know?

CUSTOMER 1 Can you tell me who designed it?

SALES ASSISTANT Yes, it ² _____ (design) by Ringo Starr and Robin Cruikshank in the 1970s.

CUSTOMER 1 Ringo Starr? From The Beatles?

SALES ASSISTANT Yes, that's right.

CUSTOMER 2 Hello there. I'm interested in the 1960s coat rack on your website.

SALES ASSISTANT Erm, which one?

CUSTOMER 2 It ³ _____ (made of) wood and metal.

SALES ASSISTANT Ah, yes. I know the one. Do you need any more information about it?

CUSTOMER 2 Yes, actually. ⁴ _____ (design) in Britain?

SALES ASSISTANT No, it wasn't. It ⁵ _____ (design) in Germany, in the 1960s.

CUSTOMER 3 Hello. I'm calling about the 1950s wardrobe on your website – the one with the blue doors.

SALES ASSISTANT Yes, how can I help?

CUSTOMER 3 Where ⁶ _____ (make)?

SALES ASSISTANT It ⁷ _____ (make) in the UK by a company called Lebetkin Furniture.

7 Match the sentence parts to make phrases for talking about a possession.

1	(It) helps	a	since/for ...
2	My favourite	b	love it because ...
3	It was	c	given to me by ...
4	It's	d	made of ...
5	I've had it	e	of ...
6	I need it	f	me to ...
7	I absolutely	g	for ...
8	It reminds me	h	thing is ...

8 Branko is talking about his favourite possession. Complete the text with the expressions from Exercise 7.

I think ¹*my favourite thing is* my 1970s record player.
² _____ beautiful old wood, and
³ _____ I was 15. ⁴ _____
my father, and ⁵ _____ him.
Some of my friends think that I'm crazy to still play records,
but ⁶ _____ I think records sound better than
MP3s. I have an MP3 player, too, of course –
⁷ _____ when I go to work or on holiday –
but playing records ⁸ _____ relax, especially
after a stressful day at the office.

Branko, Serbia

Over to you

Write about your favourite possession. Use the expressions in Exercise 7.

MYEnglish

9 Ainhoa, from Spain, is studying at a summer school in England. Read her conversation with her teacher, Matt, and answer the questions.

1 What did Ainhoa want to buy from the market?
2 What mistake did Ainhoa make?

AINHOA Can I ask you about something strange that happened to me this morning?

MATT Yes, of course.

AINHOA Well, I was in the market and I wanted to buy a T-shirt. The stallholder gave me a blue one, so I said 'No, I want the red *one*.'

MATT OK.

AINHOA But the man didn't understand me. Did I say the wrong thing?

MATT Well, you said the right thing, but you used the wrong stress. You said 'No, I want the red *one*', with the stress on *one*.

AINHOA Is that not correct? In Spanish, it sounds correct.

MATT No, you should stress the word that's important.

AINHOA So I should say 'No, I want the *red* one'?

MATT Yes, that's right!

Your English

10 Think about these questions.

1 Do you think Ainhoa's mistake was serious?
2 Have you ever made a mistake like Ainhoa's? What happened?

11 Contrastive stress can help to emphasise what's important. <u>Underline</u> the words in these sentences that have contrastive stress. Then practise saying the sentences.

1 No, I want the <u>green</u> one. *(Not the red one.)*
2 Jan's wearing the blue T-shirt. *(Not the blue jumper.)*
3 Can I see the smaller one? *(Not the larger one.)*
4 Carlos is sitting next to Adam. *(Not sitting next to Ben.)*
5 Carlos is sitting next to Adam. *(Not standing next to Adam.)*

EXPLOREWriting

12 Read the advert from an online auction website. Are these sentences true or false?

1 The seller found the vase in his grandmother's house in 1956. TRUE / ~~FALSE~~
2 The company who made the vase aren't in business any more. TRUE / FALSE
3 The seller is happy to sell the vase. TRUE / FALSE
4 The seller is selling the vase because he needs the money. TRUE / FALSE
5 The seller will pay the costs of posting the vase to the buyer. TRUE / FALSE

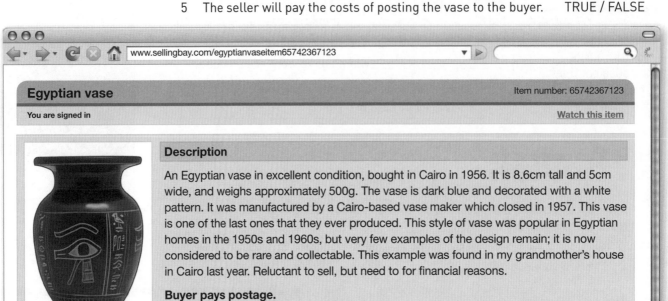

www.sellingbay.com/egyptianvaseitem65742367123

Egyptian vase   Item number: 65742367123

You are signed in   Watch this item

Description

An Egyptian vase in excellent condition, bought in Cairo in 1956. It is 8.6cm tall and 5cm wide, and weighs approximately 500g. The vase is dark blue and decorated with a white pattern. It was manufactured by a Cairo-based vase maker which closed in 1957. This vase is one of the last ones that they ever produced. This style of vase was popular in Egyptian homes in the 1950s and 1960s, but very few examples of the design remain; it is now considered to be rare and collectable. This example was found in my grandmother's house in Cairo last year. Reluctant to sell, but need to for financial reasons.

Buyer pays postage.

Thank you, please see my other auctions!

13 Find words or expressions in the advert with the following meanings.

1 in a very good state; not damaged = _in excellent condition_
2 8.6 by 5 centimetres = _____
3 about; more or less = _____
4 not pale = _____
5 the design of lines, shapes, colours, etc. = _____
6 made by = _____
7 not common; very unusual = _____
8 something that people want to collect = _____
9 not wanting to do something = _____
10 money that you pay to send a letter or parcel = _____

14 Tick (✓) the information which is included in the advert.

1 What condition the item is in ✓
2 Where and when the seller bought or found it ☐
3 How much the seller paid for the item ☐
4 How big it is ☐
5 How much it weighs ☐
6 What it looks like ☐
7 Who made it ☐
8 If it is rare or collectable, and why ☐
9 Why the seller likes the item ☐
10 Why the seller is selling it ☐
11 When the seller decided to sell it ☐
12 Who pays for the postage ☐

15 Think of an item that you could sell on an online auction site. Write a description of the item, using some or all of the information in Exercise 14.

1 Before you watch, think about this question: do you have a favourite possession? What is it?

2 Watch the video. Match the favourite possessions (a–c) with the speakers (1–3).

Anna Laura   Justyna   Laura

3 Write AL (Anna Laura), J (Justyna) or L (Laura). Watch again to check.

Whose favourite possession ...

1 ... belonged to her grandmother? _____J_____

2 ... was an anniversary present? _____

3 ... was bought in Italy? _____

4 ... has been in the family for many years? _____

5 ... has helped her to have many wonderful experiences? _____

6 ... makes her think of a happy time? _____

7 ... makes her think of things she will do in the future? _____

4 Complete the sentences from the video using a word from each box.

allowed   been   brings   ~~made~~   shape   back   in   ~~of~~   of   to

1 I think it's _made_ _of_ enamel and the design is called Klimt Design.

2 I think it's really pretty, but perhaps more importantly it _____ _____ all the memories of being there.

3 It's a little brooch in the _____ _____ a sunflower.

4 It has _____ _____ my family for many years.

5 It's _____ me _____ see so many wonderful places and meet so many wonderful people.

5 Write about your favourite possession. Use these questions to help you.

1 Where or who did you get it from?
2 What is it made of?
3 Is it in the shape of anything?
4 Does it bring back any memories?
5 Has it been in your family for a long time?
6 Has it allowed you to do anything special or interesting?

GLOSSARY

enamel (noun): shiny, hard paint for decorating metal
possession (noun): something you own, that is yours
pin (verb): to attach something with a pin (a thin piece of metal with a sharp point)
wedding anniversary (noun): the date you remember or celebrate the day you got married
wonderful (adjective): very good, excellent

9 Feelings

VOCABULARY

Extreme
adjectives

1 Match the ordinary adjectives (1–8) with the extreme adjectives (a–h).

1	angry	a	amazed
2	cold	b	boiling
3	frightened	c	delighted
4	hot	d	exhausted
5	hungry	e	freezing
6	pleased	f	furious
7	surprised	g	starving
8	tired	h	terrified

2 Complete the conversations with adjectives from Exercise 1.

1

Are you pleased with your new house?

Oh yes, we're really _delighted_ . It's lovely.

2

The boss is looking for you. He's really furious about that file you lost.

Oh no, I knew he'd be _____ .

3

Can we stop and eat our sandwiches now?

Good idea. I'm absolutely _____ .

4

Sure. I'll do it.

Could we shut the window? It's absolutely _____ in here.

5

You were very brave to speak at the conference.

Yes, I was absolutely _____ , but it went really well.

6

Are you coming to the reception after work?

No, sorry. I'm really _____ . I'm going to go straight home to bed!

7

I was very surprised to hear that Frank's getting married.

I was absolutely _____ ! But I'm sure they'll be happy together.

8

Be careful with the water. It can be a bit hot.

Aaagh, yes! It's absolutely _____ .

44

VOCABULARY

Reacting to
news, thanking,
apologising

3 Cross out the expressions that are *not* appropriate responses.

1 **A** I'm really angry. Someone's just taken my bike from outside my house!
  B That's not good. / ~~That's very kind of you.~~ / I'm really sorry.
2 **A** Wow! I got it! I got the job!
  B You're welcome! / Congratulations! / Well done!
3 **A** I got these flowers for you in the market. I thought you'd like them.
  B Thanks very much. / Don't mention it. / That's very kind of you.
4 **A** Oh, thank you. They're lovely. That's very kind of you.
  B Don't mention it. / You're welcome. / Well done.
5 **A** What happened? Why are you so late?
  B I'm really sorry. / I'd like to apologise. / I'm sorry to hear that.

GRAMMAR

The present
perfect 3 –
giving news

4 Match the sentences.

1 They've moved house.
2 They've opened a new office.
3 She's just had another baby.
4 They've given the job to someone else.
5 I've finished writing the report.
6 He's broken his foot.
7 I've bought a new jacket.
8 I've done the shopping.
9 He's failed his exams.

a He can't play in the match tomorrow.
b She's really furious.
c I can give it to you tomorrow.
d They've got four children now.
e He'll have to do them again in September.
f There will be 70 new jobs.
g They live in Scotland now.
h I'm going to wear it for the party.
i I got most of the things on the list.

5 Complete Sinead's email to her friend Trish. Use the present perfect of the verbs in the box.

~~buy~~ find have learn make open start visit

Hi!

Sorry it's such a long time since I wrote to you, but we've been really busy since we moved here.

When we arrived, we stayed in a flat in the centre, but now we ¹ *'ve bought* a house with a little garden just outside the town. Kieran ² _____ working and is enjoying the atmosphere in the office. I ³ _____ a job, too – I'm starting next week! It's in a new jewellery shop that ⁴ _____ in the old market building.

The children don't start school until September, but they ⁵ _____ friends with the kids next door – they think it's great here!

We ⁶ _____ a few trips to the beach at the weekends, and we ⁷ _____ to windsurf – yes, all of us! I was terrified at first, but it's good fun. And we ⁸ _____ some of the other towns near here. It's a really pretty area, so you have to come to see us!

VOCABULARY
Asking for news

Over to you

What's new with you? Write three pieces of news to tell a friend.

6 At the end of her email, Sinead asks Trish for her news. Put the words in the correct order.

Anyway, ¹with / what's / you / new / ? _____

²you / to / What / been / have / up _____ since we left?

³James / kids / How / the / and / are / ? _____ I hope
they're all OK. And ⁴work / how / at / are / things / ? _____

Are you still in the HR department? Say hello to everyone for me!

Write soon and tell me your news.

Love

Sinead

Time**Out**

7 Are these statements true or false?

1 Pet dogs often yawn because their human companions do.   TRUE / FALSE

2 Yawning when you are on a plane that's landing can make your ears hurt.   TRUE / FALSE

3 People often make eye contact when they give you a false smile.   TRUE / FALSE

4 Humans are the only animals that smile when they are happy.   TRUE / FALSE

5 In the native American Navajo tradition, people have a party for a baby's first laugh.   TRUE / FALSE

6 The scientific study of laughter is called 'gelotology'.   TRUE / FALSE

7 Sudden bright light can make people sneeze.   TRUE / FALSE

8 Everyone closes their eyes when they sneeze.   TRUE / FALSE

EXPLOREReading

8 Read the introduction to this online article about how we show our feelings. Are the sentences true or false?

1 Experts all believe that fear and love are basic human emotions. **TRUE / FALSE**
2 Emotions are shown by people's words and by the signs their bodies give. **TRUE / FALSE**
3 It's a useful social skill to know how to recognise people's feelings. **TRUE / FALSE**

Feelings

What are the basic emotions? Experts disagree, but most agree that they include: anger, sadness, surprise, joy or happiness, fear or anxiety. Some also include interest, and love or affection.

With careful observation, emotions may be detected from non-verbal signs. Remember that these are indicators, not certain signs. You can also use the context, in particular what people are saying or what is happening around the person.

Learn to recognise emotions. If you can see the emotion, then you can respond to it appropriately.

Anger
We become angry when we can't do what we want.
✦ Our neck and/or face is red.
✦ Our teeth are shown.
✦ We close our hands into fists.
✦ Our body leans forward and invades other people's space.
✦ Aggressive body language (like sudden or loud movements) is used.

Surprise
We are surprised when things happen which we did not expect.
✦ Our eyebrows go up.
✦ Our eyes open wide.
✦ Our mouth opens.
✦ Our body moves backwards.

Happiness
We feel happy when we have what we want.
✦ Our muscles are relaxed.
✦ We smile.
✦ We use open body language.

Sadness
Sadness is the opposite of happiness, and indicates a depressive state.
✦ Our body 'drops' downwards.
✦ We use a flat tone of voice when we speak.
✦ We cry.

Fear
Being frightened is a very basic emotion. There are many levels of fear, from worry or anxiety to real terror. The changes in our bodies when we are frightened make it easy to see.
✦ Our face is white or pale.
✦ Our mouth is dry; we may lick our lips or drink water.
✦ We don't look at the other person.
✦ Our eyes are wet.
✦ Our voice shakes, and we make errors when we speak.
✦ Our pulse rate is fast.
✦ We sweat; this can be a 'cold sweat'.
✦ Our muscles are tense.
✦ Our breathing is irregular.
✦ We change body position a lot.
✦ Defensive body language (like crossing our arms) is used.

9 Read the rest of the article and circle the correct way to complete the sentences.

1 When people are angry, they may move forward / backward, and their face is often pale / red.
2 Someone who is surprised has open / closed eyes and an open / a closed mouth.
3 A happy person probably opens / crosses their arms.
4 A sad person probably speaks quietly / loudly.
5 It is easy / difficult to understand when people are frightened.
6 Someone who is frightened probably looks / doesn't look at you, and moves / doesn't move a lot.

10 Match the phrases from the article (1–6) with the correct picture (a–f).

1 We may lick our lips. `a`
2 We close our hands into fists. ☐
3 We sweat. ☐
4 We use open body language. ☐
5 Our body drops downwards. ☐
6 Our eyebrows go up. ☐

DVD-ROM Extra Ways of communicating

1   Before you watch, think about this question: in your culture, when people communicate, do they use a lot of gestures and body language?

2   Watch the video. Who talks about communicating in these ways? Write S (Shih-chen), P (Paivi) or S/P (both).

Shih-chen Paivi

1   using body language   _P_
2   using facial expressions   _____
3   using their hands   _____
4   writing and drawing   _____
5   using gesture   _____

3   Are these sentences true or false? Watch Shih-chen again (00:12–01:17) to check.

1   Shih-chen stayed in a kind of bed and breakfast in Tokyo.   TRUE / FALSE
2   The man in the bed and breakfast spoke some English and Mandarin. TRUE / FALSE
3   The Japanese and Chinese languages use the same written characters. TRUE / FALSE
4   Shih-chen drew maps to communicate with the man.   TRUE / FALSE

4   Complete the extracts using the words in the box. Watch Shih-chen again (00:12–01:17) to check.

> how   what   ~~when~~   where   which   why

1   _When_ I was in Tokyo on my own ...
2   I just lived in this *ryokan*, _____ is like a bed and breakfast.
3   The reason _____ we could use the Chinese characters to communicate ...
4   ... so that's _____ I did.
5   I had no idea _____ to get there.
6   This is _____ I wanted to go.

5   (Circle) the correct words to complete the summary of what Paivi says about using body language. Watch the video again (01:23–02:29) to check.

When she went to Scotland, Paivi [1]was / wasn't surprised that people [2]used / didn't use a lot of body language. She [3]thought / didn't think body language was used more by people from Latin America, France and Italy. When she went home to Finland, she noticed that people [4]used / didn't use body language in the same way.

6   Complete what Paivi says about her feelings and ideas using the words in the box.

> fascinated   had this image   looking at   ~~noticed~~   surprised   thinking   thought

1   The first thing I _noticed_ was ...
2   And I was quite _____ because ...
3   I _____ in my head ...
4   I just was _____ ...
5   I was _____ people on the street.
6   ... _____ this is very different from what I _____ it would be.

7   Have you noticed people from different cultures using different gestures and body language?

GLOSSARY

facial (adjective): on your face
characters (plural noun): Some languages, like Chinese and Japanese, use written symbols, or **characters**, instead of an alphabet.
tourist spot (noun): a place that tourists like to go to
eyebrows (plural noun): the lines of hair above your eyes
shrug (verb): You **shrug** your shoulders to show you don't know something or you're not interested.

Getting organised

10

VOCABULARY
Hotel facilities

1 Complete the hotel facilities.

Hotel facilities

🏊 swimming pool   🛏 meeting rooms

AC ¹ a _i r_ _c o n d i t i o n i n g_   👕 ⁴ l _ _ _ _ _ _ _

🍸 bar   📺 cable/satellite TV

🍴 ² r _ _ _ _ _ _ _ _ _ _   💻 business centre

🏋 ³ h _ _ _ _ _ _ c _ _ _ _   📶 ⁵ w _ _ _ _ _ _ _ _ _
i _ _ _ _ _ _ _ _ _
a _ _ _ _ _ _

---

2 Complete the extract from a hotel's website using the words in the box.

> air conditioned   business centre   health club   laundry service
> ~~parking~~   restaurants   wireless internet

Located in the heart of Santiago, the Honister Santiago Hotel is just 20 minutes from the airport and an easy drive from the beach. If you are arriving by car, the hotel has secure
¹ ___parking___ for 350 cars.

Families can splash around in the indoor and outdoor swimming pools, keep fit at our
² _____, or share a meal with friends at our three famous ³ _____.

Relax in one of our range of double, twin and single rooms. All rooms are ⁴ _____, modern and luxurious, and each has ⁵ _____ access – absolutely free.

Our ⁶ _____ will be happy to deliver your clean clothes to your room.

If you're here to do business, you'll find the ⁷ _____ on the second floor with state-of-the-art technology and multilingual staff to help you.

Over to you

When you choose a hotel, which facilities are important to you? Make a list.

VOCABULARY
Staying in a hotel

3 Decide who says each thing, the receptionist (R) or the guest (G).

1 Sorry, could you spell your surname for me, please? [R]

2 Do you have a map of the city, please? ☐

3 Do I have to sign the form twice? ☐

4 What time is breakfast? ☐

5 Would you like some help with your bags? ☐

a It's OK, thanks, I can carry them myself. ☐

b Yes, please. And can I see your passport, please? ☐

c Of course. It's R-A-M-O-S. ☐

d Yes, here you are. There's also some information in your room. ☐

e It's from 7.00 to 11.00 in the restaurant downstairs. ☐

4 Match the questions in Exercise 3 (1–5) with the answers (a–e).

5 How connected are you? Circle your answer to each question.

HOW CONNECTED ARE YOU?

1 You are talking to a friend when you hear your mobile beep to tell you that you have a new message. You:
A read it immediately and write your answer.
B say 'Excuse me', quickly look at your new message, then put your phone back in your pocket.
C ignore it. You can read it later.

2 How many internet 'friends' do you have?
A Lots! I have online friends all over the world.
B I have some online friends, but they're not *real* friends.
C I don't understand the question. How can you have friends on the Internet?

3 After your birthday party, you want to show the photographs to your friends. You:
A post them on your social networking site.
B send copies to your friends by email.
C print your photos and then put them in an album to show to your friends.

4 You and your partner decide to get married. You:
A announce it on your social networking site for all your friends on the Internet to see.
B telephone your friends to tell them the good news.
C arrange a meeting with all your friends to tell them about your plan.

5 It's your best friend's birthday. You:
A send an e-card to say 'Happy Birthday'.
B buy a nice card and post it to your friend.
C make a card and arrange to meet your friend to hand it over.

Answers

Mostly As: You love new technology and you're well connected around the world. But remember that you have to move away from your keyboard and talk to your friends face to face sometimes!

Mostly Bs: You have a good balance between using new technology and keeping the personal touch.

Mostly Cs: Talking to people face to face is very important to you. You're not keen on new technology – but remember that it can also help you keep in touch with your friends.

6 Complete these sentences using the best form of the verb in brackets. Sometimes more than one verb form is possible.

1 My train ___*arrives*___ (arrive) at five o'clock.
2 We _____ (go) to Spain next summer to visit my brother.
3 My boss wants to talk about the report. We _____ (meet) at three o'clock.
4 She _____ (be) a teacher when she finishes college.
5 There _____ (be) a really good film on TV tonight.

7 Write true answers to these questions.

1 What are you doing next weekend?
2 What are you going to have for dinner tonight?
3 What are you going to do tomorrow?
4 Where are you going for your next holiday?

VOCABULARY

make

make a lot of money
make a mistake
~~make a presentation~~
make arrangements
make dinner
make new friends

8 Complete the sentences using the expressions with *make* in the box.

1 I had to _make a presentation_ to 50 people at work on Monday. I was really nervous.
2 Don't worry if you _____. Just cross it out and start again.
3 OK, I'll go to the supermarket and get everything we need, and you can _____.
4 I don't _____, but I really enjoy my work.
5 I'm quite shy, so I don't find it easy to _____.
6 We need to _____ for the conference. How many people are coming?

MYEnglish

9 Read the page from Jung-Soo's blog. Tick (✓) the things Jung-Soo has done to help him learn English.

⦿ ⦿ ⦿ ⬭

BLOG SPOT

There are lots of places to learn English here in Korea. I had English lessons at school and I also went to a private language school in the evenings. But the place I really learnt English was on the Internet. Most people in Korea use the Internet a lot, but without English, it's difficult to really connect with the whole world.

I know some great sites for learning English, with exercises and activities. I read some English newspapers online and – most important for me – I chat in English with people from all over the world.

It can be difficult to find people to speak English to in real life, but on the Internet, I can speak to interesting people everywhere. I've made some really good friends through the Internet and English.

1	attended classes	✓	4 done online exercises	☐
2	studied books	☐	5 chatted to people online in English	☐
3	read online newspapers	☐		

Your English

10 Lots of the words Jung-Soo uses to talk about computers are also used in Korean, as 'loan words' from English. They are English words that are also used in Korean.

All these words are similar in Korean to the English word. How do you say them in your language?

English	Your language
computer	_____
email	_____
file	_____
Internet	_____
keyboard	_____
monitor	_____
mouse	_____
printer	_____
programme	_____
website	_____

11 Can you think of any other loan words in your language?

12 Which of the things from Exercise 9 have you done?

attended classes ☐	read online newspapers ☐	chatted to people online in English ☐
studied books ☐	done online exercises ☐	

13 What websites do you know that can help you learn English? Search online and make notes.

• Exercises and learning activities • Online news in English

EXPLOREWriting

Maike, Australia

14 Maike is arranging a surprise birthday party for her dad. Read her email to her brother, Joe. Who is arriving when? Match the names (1–3) with the days (a–c).

1	Pete	a	Thursday night
2	Joe	b	Friday morning
3	Ally	c	Friday afternoon

Delete Reply Reply All Forward Print

Hi Joe!

Dad still doesn't know anything about the party. He'll be so surprised to see you all. I can't wait to see his face.

Here's the plan so far:

Ally is going to drive up from Melbourne on Thursday night. She's staying with Uncle Bob and Auntie Kate. Pete, Kumiko and the kids are coming on Friday morning. Pete says he'll come to the airport and pick you up. What time does your flight arrive? You're staying with Meg and Ryan – I hope that's OK.

I'm going to make a big cake, and Ally's made a big flag that says 'HAPPY 60th, DAD' that she's going to bring with her on Thursday. She sent me a photo, and it looks great.

Remember, Dad usually gets back from his game of golf at 12 on Saturdays. We all have to be there by 11.30.

Anyway, we can make all the other arrangements when we see each other.

See you on Friday

Love

Maike

15 Find examples in the email of these tenses for future arrangements.

1 Three examples of the present progressive for arrangements that have been made with people.
2 Three examples of *be going to* + infinitive for personal plans.
3 One example of the present simple for things with fixed times.

16 Imagine you have planned a surprise party for someone in your family. Write an email to a friend or relative saying what the arrangements are.

• Who is coming and when are they arriving?
• What is arranged for the party? Who is doing what?
• Are there other important parts of the plan?

1   Before you watch, think about this question: are you still in touch with your school friends?
How do you keep in touch with them?

2   Watch the video and choose the best way to complete the sentences.

Monica

Rushda

1   Monica mainly uses the Internet to ...
   a)   look for holidays abroad.
   b)   make new friends.
   c)   stay in touch with old friends.
2   Rushda now mainly uses the Internet to ...
   a)   write to her brother.
   b)   write her blog and read her friends' comments.
   c)   meet lots of new people.

3   Who is each sentence about? Write M (Monica) or R (Rushda). Watch again to check.

1   Some of her friends live abroad.   _____

2   She was one of the first internet users.   _____

3   She used to go to chatrooms a lot.   _____

4   She sends photos to her friends.   _____

4   Monica and Rushda both use words connected with computers and the Internet. Can you remember what
they said? Complete the sentences, then watch again to check.

Monica

1   Thanks to the _____ and _____ lots of _____ where you can keep in touch with

   friends, ...

2   We _____ photographs, we _____ information and we send each other _____ .

Rushda

3   So I went on _____ and talked to all kinds of people.

4   Nowadays, I don't use _____ as much. I still go on lots of _____ .

5   I even have my own _____ now and I can write my own opinions.

5   What do you usually use the Internet for? Is it different from when you first used it?

GLOSSARY

chatroom (noun): a website where you can meet and talk to different people

11 Spaces

VOCABULARY

Describing homes

1 Match the features (a–h) to the pictures (1–8).

a wooden floors ☐ 8
b garden ☐
c parking ☐
d air conditioning ☐
e fireplace ☐
f balcony ☐
g barbecue ☐
h swimming pool ☐

2 Rearrange the letters in the adjectives in bold to complete the advert.

Over to you

Which of the features in Exercise 1 would be most important for you if you were looking for a house or apartment? Put the list in order (1 = the most important).

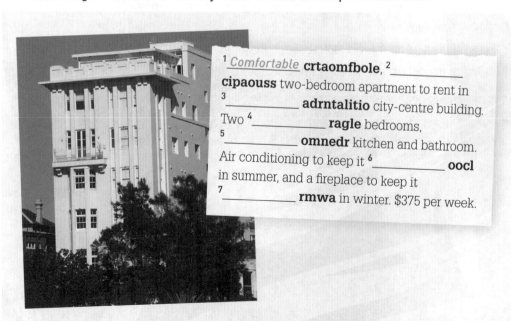

¹ _Comfortable_ **crtaomfbole**, ² _____ **cipaouss** two-bedroom apartment to rent in ³ _____ **adrntalitio** city-centre building. Two ⁴ _____ **ragle** bedrooms, ⁵ _____ **omnedr** kitchen and bathroom. Air conditioning to keep it ⁶ _____ **oocl** in summer, and a fireplace to keep it ⁷ _____ **rmwa** in winter. $375 per week.

3 Nikos and Jessica have been to see the apartment in Exercise 2. Choose the correct words to complete their conversation.

NIKOS	So, what did you think?
JESSICA	Well, the ¹best / worst thing about it is the location: it's right in the city centre, which would be great.
NIKOS	Yeah, but the ²good / bad thing about living in the centre is the noise.
JESSICA	The ³best thing / trouble is, if we want to live closer to your office, then we're going to have to put up with some extra noise.
NIKOS	I know. The ⁴good thing / thing is, I'm not sure really I want to live closer to work.
JESSICA	But what about your long journey to the office?
NIKOS	Well, the ⁵good / bad thing about commuting is that I get to read a lot – and I can sleep on the train!
JESSICA	Fine, then! We'll stay where we are.

4 Look at the definition of an *agony aunt*. Do you have agony aunts in your country?

agony aunt *noun* [C] someone who gives advice on personal problems, in a newspaper or magazine

Anya, UK

5 Anya has written to an online agony aunt, where other readers can make suggestions on how to solve your problem. Read Anya's post. What is her problem?

1 She doesn't like living with Fiona.
2 She doesn't like living with Melissa.
3 She doesn't like living in that apartment.

Advice Online.org

ANYA:

I live in a small two-bedroom apartment with one other girl, my flatmate Fiona. Three weeks ago, one of Fiona's friends came to visit from the USA, a girl called Melissa. Now Melissa's practically moved in! She's using our living room as a bedroom, so I can't use that room to relax or watch TV. And she's really messy: she never washes the dishes after she's cooked.

Yesterday, Fiona asked if Melissa could stay with us for a couple of months. I want to say no, but I don't want to upset Fiona. I love living in this apartment, and I don't want to move out. What should I do?

6 Several readers have posted suggestions for Anya. Complete them using the words in the box.

Could 'd 'd should Would

Do you have a suggestion? Post your comments below.

NIKEY:
¹ _Could_ you ask Melissa to be tidier – you know, to wash some dishes occasionally?

UNKNOWN:
Maybe you ²_____ look for somewhere else to live. It sounds like your flatmate is quite selfish.

KELVIN:
I ³_____ probably ask Melissa to pay some rent if she's going to stay for a couple of months. It's only fair.

MATEITO:
⁴_____ it be possible for Fiona and Melissa to share Fiona's room? That way, you'd be able to use the living room again.

LADY ENIGMA:
I ⁵_____ tell Melissa to make less mess or move out – it's her choice.

7 Write a piece of advice for Anya.

_____

_____

Time**Out**

8 Complete the crossword.

ACROSS
3 not too hot, but not too cold
4 with a lot of space
5 space in the wall where you can have a fire
7 the opposite of 3 Across
8 leaving your car somewhere
10 used for cooking food outdoors
11 in an up-to-date style

DOWN
1 the opposite of 11 Across
2 not small
6 small area on the side of a building where you can stand or sit
9 usually contains grass, flowers, trees, etc.

EXPLORE Reading

9   When you want to buy or rent a property, the estate agent shows you the property details. Read the property details for 67 North Street. How many rooms does the house have, not including the entrance hall?

67 North Street

Situated close to the city centre and railway station, this three-bedroom house is decorated to a high standard <u>throughout</u> and offers full <u>double glazing</u>, separate WC, and modern <u>kitchen/diner</u>.

Lounge 4.32m x 4.93m
Fireplace, double-glazed front-facing window and radiator.

Entrance hall
Double-glazed entrance door, radiator, double-glazed window, staircase to first floor.

Kitchen 3.94m x 4.93m
<u>Fully fitted</u> kitchen, <u>built-in</u> electric oven, built-in gas <u>hob</u>, space for dishwasher.

Separate WC
WC and <u>hand basin</u>.

Bedroom 1 4.85m x 2.51m
Double-glazed front-facing window and radiator.

Bedroom 2 3.07m x 2.51m
Double-glazed rear-facing window and radiator.

Bedroom 3 2.26m x 2.26m
Double-glazed front-facing window and radiator.

Bathroom 2.07m x 2.26m
<u>Tiled</u> bath with shower, hand basin, WC, extractor fan, heated towel rail and double-glazed rear-facing window.

Front garden
Mainly <u>paved</u>.

Rear garden
Large <u>lawn</u>.

10   Read the property details again and answer these questions.

1   Which is the biggest room in the house?   _the lounge_
2   How many toilets does the house have?   _____
3   Find at least two things that would keep the house warm in the winter.
     _____   _____
4   If you are standing in bedroom 2, which garden can you see?   _____
5   If you are standing in bedroom 3, which garden can you see?   _____

11   Find <u>underlined</u> words in the property details with the following meanings.

1   a room where you can cook and also eat   _kitchen/diner_
2   covered with stones, bricks, concrete, etc.   _____
3   the part of the garden which is grass   _____
4   the top of an oven where you heat food   _____
5   everywhere   _____
6   part of something   _____
7   windows that have two layers of glass to keep a building warm or quiet
     _____
8   where you can wash your hands   _____
9   designed and built for this space   _____
10 covered with small square pieces of ceramic or plastic   _____

12   Why would 67 North Street probably *not* be suitable for these people?

1   Hugh and Tracey Metcalf have four teenage children and are looking for a centrally located house with lots of outdoor space.
2   Cathryn Reese is 89 years old and has some trouble walking. She wants at least two bedrooms, a nice kitchen and a small garden.
3   Craig and Marta Caputo have a two-year-old child, Ana. They're looking for a house in a quiet location. Craig and Marta both work from home.

1   Before you watch, think about a time you moved to a new house, town or country. Was it a good or bad experience?

2   Watch Salvatore and Vesna. Answer the questions by writing S (Salvatore) or V (Vesna).

Who ...

1   ... went to a place to help a family member?   _____

2   ... went to live in a new country?   _____

3   ... felt like a different person after the experience?   _____

4   ... felt happy and satisfied after their experience?   _____

Salvatore

Vesna

3   Watch Salvatore again (00:11–01:13). Match the beginnings and endings of the phrases to make time expressions.

1   A few years
2   As soon
3   ... we had to sleep there, um, obviously during
4   In the

a   as we arrived there, we realised that, um, windows need to be changed, ...
b   the night, and this was during winter and ...
c   end, the house was beautiful and refurbished, and the satisfaction was great for it.
d   ago, my uncle and I decided to refurbish my grandfather's house.

4   Look at the sentences in Exercise 3 again. Which verb form do we use after the expressions *a few years ago*, *as soon as* and *in the end*?

5   Watch Vesna again (01:19–03:08). For each of these extracts, decide if she is talking about something positive (P) or something negative (N).

1 ... it was winter time and, ah, it _was_ (be) cold, and, ah, lots of snow around. No people. We _____ (be) sort of, ah, very lonely. ☐

2 We _____ (be) just, just us and this Finnish coldness and darkness there, everything like death. ☐

3 ... later on I, I _____ (study) Finnish and meet many nice people at the university and we gradually _____ (become) friends and, ah, I _____ (learn) to love Finnish food and ... ☐

4 ... and everything that I _____ (hate) at the beginning I _____ (start) really loving. ☐

5 ... and, ah, I _____ (change) myself as well. I _____ (become) sort of Serbian Finnish person and even nowadays, I, I, I like telling that I am not really a Serbian person but something in between Serbian and Finnish. ☐

6   Complete the extracts in Exercise 5 with the correct form of the verbs in brackets. Watch again to check.

7   What verb form are all of the verbs in Exercise 6? Why?

8   Write about the experience you thought about in Exercise 1. Use the correct verb forms.

GLOSSARY

Finnish (adjective): the adjective from the country Finland
inland (adjective): not near the coast
refurbish (verb): to improve or repair a building
satisfaction (noun): a good feeling when you have done something you wanted to do
Serbian (adjective): the adjective from the country Serbia
work in progress: If something is **a work in progress**, it is not yet complete.

12 People and places

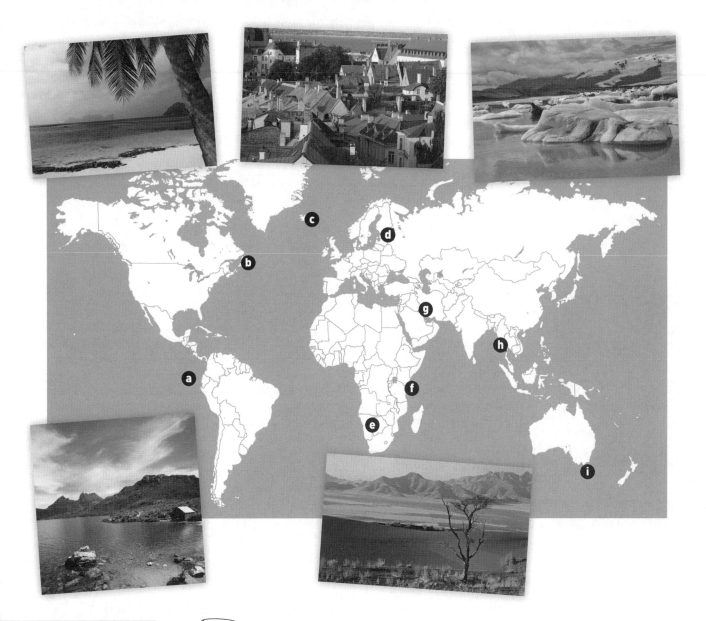

1 (Circle) the correct words.

1 The Andaman Islands are a group / coast of islands in the Indian Ocean. [h]
2 Estonia is in north / the north of Europe, and it borders / between Latvia
   and Russia.
3 Tasmania is a large island / coast to the south-east of / south-east Australia.
4 Kuwait is in the Middle East between / in the west of Saudi Arabia and Iraq.
5 Newfoundland is an island off the east coast of / coast Canada.
6 Zanzibar is an island in / on the Indian Ocean to the east / coast of Tanzania.
7 Namibia is in south-west Africa, on the Atlantic border / coast.
8 Iceland is an island nation / place in the Norwegian Sea.
9 The Galapagos Islands are in the Pacific to the west of / west Ecuador.

2 How good is your geography? Look at the map and match the places in Exercise 1
with the countries (a–i).

3 Write the letter of each place (a–i) beside the correct continent.

Europe _c_ ___   Australasia ___   Africa ___ ___

Asia ___ ___   South America ___   North America ___

4 Read the first paragraph of the text about Malta and answer the questions about its location.

1 Which continent is Malta in? _____
2 Which sea is it in? _____

5 Read all the text and complete the facts about Malta using the words in the box.

capital famous independent member money
official languages past population

1 _The capital is_ Valletta.
2 _____ about 400,000.
3 _____ Maltese and English.
4 _____ the EU, the British Commonwealth and the UN.
5 It _____ from manufacturing, services and tourism.
6 In _____, it was ruled by the Greeks, Romans and Phoenicians.
7 It _____ in 1964.
8 It's _____ its ancient temples and beautiful beaches.

EUROPE

Malta

The Republic of Malta is an island nation. It is made up of seven islands, the largest being Malta, Gozo and Comino. The capital, Valletta, is on the main island of Malta. The islands are in the south of Europe, 93 kilometres south of the coast of Sicily in the Mediterranean. It is also very close to Africa – Tunisia is less than 300 km away – and has a typical Mediterranean climate, with mild winters and very hot summers.

People first came to these islands from Sicily over 7,000 years ago, and there are remains of many other civilisations, including Greek, Roman, Phoenician and Arab. It has several large stone temples, which are the oldest monuments in the world.

Nowadays, it has a population of about 400,000 people. The official languages are Maltese and English, but Italian is spoken by many people, too. It gained independence from Britain in 1964 and joined the European Union in 2004. It is also a member of the British Commonwealth and the United Nations.

Malta does not have very much agriculture. Many people work in manufacturing and service industries, but tourism is one of the largest sources of income. Over 1 million people visit the country every year, attracted by its rich history and culture, and its beautiful beaches.

6 Match the sentence halves to find out about the life and achievements of Dr Mae Jemison.

1 She was born
2 She became interested in
3 She always wanted to
4 She went to Stanford University
5 She qualified
6 She joined
7 She was the first black woman
8 She acted in

a science when she was a child.
b as a medical doctor in 1981.
c an episode of _Star Trek: The Next Generation_!
d to go into space, in 1992.
e in Alabama in 1956.
f at the age of only 16.
g go into space.
h NASA in 1987.

7 Here is some more information about Mae Jemison. Circle the correct way to complete the sentences.

1 She became interested in science by studying / to study nature.
2 She wanted becoming / to become a professional dancer.
3 She decided studying / to study science, but kept dance as a hobby.
4 She went to university studying / to study chemical engineering.
5 After qualifying / to qualify as a doctor, she worked in Cambodia and West Africa.
6 She started her own company, the Jemison Group, after leaving / to leave NASA.
7 She is interested in improving / to improve health care in developing countries.
8 She hopes continuing / to continue her work in education.

VOCABULARY
Expressions with *know*

8 Write *know* in the correct place in the sentences.

      know

1 Do you Λ anything about Che Guevara?
2 You probably that he fought in the Cuban revolution.
3 I don't much about his early life.
4 I that he was born in Argentina.
5 I don't really for sure, but I think he worked as a doctor.
6 As far as I, he spent most of his adult life in Cuba.
7 I don't when he died, but I it was in Bolivia.

MYEnglish

9 Read what these people say about languages in their countries.

Alejandra, Colombia

1 Which language connects a whole continent?
2 In which country do students study their school and university subjects in English?
3 Which country uses two major languages which are not English?
4 Which country's people use English when they travel outside their country?

> The first official language of my country is Arabic, and about 10 million people speak Berber languages, but French is also used very widely, especially in education, business and administration. So English is our third or fourth language, but it's becoming more popular, especially for young people or people who work in tourism.

> Of course, we use Spanish as our main language of communication, not only in our country, but also all through Central and South America. We learn English at school, as it's important if we want to communicate with North America or other parts of the world.

Najia, Morocco

Fabio, Italy

Daniel, Nigeria

> Italy is still a very monolingual country. Our education is in Italian, and we watch American TV programmes and movies dubbed into Italian, not in the original language. We all study English at school now, but most people only get the chance to speak English when they travel abroad.

> Nigeria has hundreds of local languages, so English is used as the official national language. Education is mostly in the English language, so we have a high standard of English for communication in our country.

Your English

10 If you are from one of the countries in Exercise 9, do you agree with the description? If your country is not here, how would you describe the use of English and other languages in your country or region?

11 A lot of English is 'international'. Here are some examples of English being used around the world. Can you think of any similar uses of English in your country?

For more practice, go to Unit 12 of the Self-study DVD-ROM.

EXPLOREWriting

LOCAL HERO AWARDS

Do you know a local hero? We are searching for people who have made a difference in your life …

- Our **Neighbour** award recognises people who make a real difference to those who live near them.
- Past or present, our **Teacher** award is for an inspirational educator, in a classroom or outside.
- Our **Boss** award is for someone who has been more than just an employer, but a friend and inspiration to colleagues.

NOMINATION FOR LOCAL HERO AWARD
LYNDA PHIPPS

1 My music teacher, Lynda Phipps, **who** has now retired, is a wonderful person and an inspirational teacher, and I would like to nominate her in the Teacher of the Year category.

2 She was born in Colchester in 1945 and she started playing the piano and organ when she was at school. **After** secondary school, she went to music college in London, **where** she met her future husband, Ian. They got married in 1967.

3 They moved to this town in 1968. While Lynda was Director of Music at the girls' school I attended, Ian **also** taught music at a local boys' school. **During** this period, they often brought students from the two schools together for concerts and informal music sessions, and in 1970, produced a performance by the two schools of a light opera. She has also organised and accompanied music trips for students to Vienna and Prague.

4 Lynda continued to teach music to children of all ages, and towards the end of her career also became the drama teacher in the school she was working in. She has been ill with multiple sclerosis for many years, **but** only retired in 2005, at the age of 60. Lynda still plays the organ in her local church and is popular in her neighbourhood. She has written and directed several musical shows, and has given the money raised from these to a local home for sick children.

5 Her lively personality and enthusiasm for music always made her lessons fun and inspiring, and she communicated a real love of music to several generations of students. I think she should have the Local Hero Teacher award.

12 Read the nomination for the Local Hero award. Are the sentences true or false?

1 Lynda Phipps taught the violin. TRUE / FALSE
2 Her husband was also a music teacher. TRUE / FALSE

13 Which paragraph(s) include this information?

a her career ___ ___
b her childhood and education ___
c who she is and her relationship to the writer ___
d why she is special ___ ___

14 Look at the nomination to see how the words in bold are used to connect parts of the text. Then use them to complete this nomination for the Local Hero award.

Marcus Groebner, **1** _____who_____ lives in my street, is a friendly and helpful neighbour to all the local residents, and I would like to nominate him for the Neighbour category of the Local Hero awards.

When he was younger, he was a naturalist and enthusiastic traveller. **2**_____ finishing high school, he studied biology at Hamburg University. He went to work in Kenya, **3**_____ he met his wife, Angela. She was **4**_____ a traveller and amateur botanist. **5**_____ the 1970s, they worked on many conservation projects together.

They returned to Germany in 1982. He retired in 1999, **6**_____ has remained active and interested in local projects. He often gives talks on ecology and conservation to local groups, and is an enthusiastic member of the 'Help your Neighbour' group in our area.

15 Think of a person you know and admire. Write their nomination for the Local Hero award. Include some information about their life and achievements, and say why they are special.

1 Before you watch, think about this question: do you know anyone who has changed their career? Do you think this is a good idea?

2 Watch Ian and Maxime talking about career changes. Who has done these jobs? Write I (Ian) or MF (Maxime's father) or I/MF for both.

Ian   Maxime

1 bank worker   _MF_

2 teacher   _____

3 art promoter   _____

4 writer   _____

5 restaurant owner   _____

3 Order these events in Ian's life. Watch the video again (00:11–01:17) to check.

☐ win a competition
☐ work as a writer
☐ stop working as a teacher
☐ do a writing course

4 How do you think Ian feels? Circle the correct sentence.

a He doesn't like being a writer and would like to go back to teaching.
b He likes being a writer, but would like to have more time to write.

5 Circle the correct words to complete the sentences. Watch Maxime again (01:23–02:08) to check.

1 Maxime's father is very / not very interested in the things he does.
2 Maxime thinks his father is typical / not typical in his attitude to work.
3 He has / hasn't finished writing his film script.

6 Watch Maxime again and complete these expressions using the words in the box.

his in in ~~like~~ on

1   he doesn't **work** _like_ everyone
2 he often changes _____ **job**
3   he firstly **worked** _____ a bank
4   **worked** _____ art
5   he is **working** _____ a script

7 Which of the jobs that they talk about do you think would be the most interesting?

GLOSSARY

MA (noun): Master of Arts, a Master's degree
involved (adjective): interested, or connected with something
quit (verb): to leave (e.g. a job or school)
promoting (verb): Someone who **promotes** artists markets them and tries to make them more popular.
script (noun): the written words of a film or TV programme

VOCABULARY

How I feel
about gadgets

1 **Put the words in the correct order to make expressions for talking about gadgets.**

1   use / I / one, / hardly / but / I / ever / have / it
   I have one, but I hardly ever use it.

2   think / I / without / would / I / it / die
   _____

3   without / it / I / live / couldn't
   _____

4   know / don't / I / them / use / to / how
   _____

5   me / need / I / have / to / with / it
   _____

6   home / I / one / have / don't / at / even
   _____

7   job / I / it / for / use / my
   _____

8   the / I / all / use / time / it
   _____

9   I / with / bother / it / don't
   _____

10   life / It / easier / makes
   _____

Over to you

Write sentences
about the five
gadgets at the top
of the page. Use
the expressions
from Exercise 1.

2 **Which expressions in Exercise 1 do you use for …**

a   gadgets you like or use?
b   gadgets you don't like or don't use very often?

VOCABULARY

Telephone expressions

3 Complete the telephone conversations with the words in the box.

> back call calling good here It's moment
> reception ~~speak~~ take that This

AIMEE	Hi, can I ¹___*speak*___ to Marijana Corbic, please?
RECEPTIONIST	Yes, who's ²_____ ?
AIMEE	³_____ Aimee Fribourg.
RECEPTIONIST	Just a ⁴_____ , please. … I'm sorry, but Marijana isn't ⁵_____ .
AIMEE	Oh, OK.
RECEPTIONIST	Do you want me to ⁶_____ a message?
AIMEE	Yes. Could you ask her to ⁷_____ me?

MATT	Hello.
BETH	Hello, is ⁸_____ Matt Craven?
MATT	Yes.
BETH	Hello, Mr Craven. ⁹_____ is Beth Cooke from Cooke and Co.
MATT	Who?
BETH	Beth Cooke. From Cooke and Co. Is this a ¹⁰_____ time to talk?
MATT	Listen, the ¹¹_____'s really bad here. I'll call you ¹²_____ later.

4 Would the following be correct (C) or incorrect (I)?

1 Instead of saying *Can I **speak** to Marijana Corbic*, Aimee said *Can I **talk** to Marijana Corbic?*   (CORRECT) / INCORRECT

2 Instead of saying ***It's** Aimee Fribourg*, Aimee said ***I'm** Aimee Fribourg*.   CORRECT / INCORRECT

3 Instead of saying *Marijana isn't **here***, the receptionist said *Marijana isn't **there***.   CORRECT / INCORRECT

4 Instead of saying *Could you ask her to **call** me?*, Aimee said *Could you ask her to **ring** me?*   CORRECT / INCORRECT

5 Instead of *Hello, is **that** Matt Craven?*, Beth said *Hello, is **this** Matt Craven?*   CORRECT / INCORRECT

6 Instead of *I'll call you **back** later*, Matt said *I'll call you later*.   CORRECT / INCORRECT

GRAMMAR

used to, would

5 Complete the web postings from childhoodbeliefs.com with *used to* or *would*. Where both are possible, use *would*.

1 I ___*used to*___ believe that if you turned the TV off when someone was on the screen, they would die! I _____ wait until there was a scene without people before turning it off.

2 When I was little, I _____ think that there were little tiny men that lived in traffic lights that turned them red, yellow and green. I thought they _____ watch to see if there were any cars before changing the lights

3 I _____ believe that songs were performed by little bands that lived in my radio. I thought they _____ wait until the name of their band was announced and then start playing!

4 I _____ think that because it was winter in Australia when it was summer in the UK, it was December in Australia when it was June in the UK! I _____ be jealous on 25 June, because I thought people in Australia were celebrating Christmas!

5 I _____ believe that when the shop on my street closed at the end of the day, the shopkeeper _____ take all the things off the shelves and take them home … only to bring them back the next morning and put them back again!

6 Correct the mistakes in these comments on Mark Glaser's web page.

HOW HAS YOUR LIFE CHANGED ONLINE?

SHARE YOUR COMMENTS:

dooby said ...

past
In the ~~before~~, I'd put all of my photos into a photo album. Those days, I store all my photos in digital format online.
Tuesday, January 06, 1:28:00 PM

andybird said ...

In the weeks before the Internet, I used to buy CDs. Nowdays, I download all of my music from iTunes.
Tuesday, January 06, 2:32:00 PM

MrMark said ...

There are more opportunities for wasting time at work than they're used to be. I do much less work than I use to!
Wednesday, January 07, 4:13:00 PM

TimeOut

7 Which of these gadgets do you think are real? Which are invented? Check your answers below.

1 The foot mouse

A computer mouse that you control using your feet.

2 Jantex MP3 shoes

A pair of shoes with a built-in MP3 player.

3 Mindflex

A game you control using your brain.

4 The coffee-table PC

A computer built into a coffee table.

5 The M500 phone watch

A mobile phone built into a watch.

6 The R350 solar-powered remote control

A TV remote control that runs on solar power, not batteries.

Over to you

Which of the gadgets from Exercise 7 would you like to own? Why? Record yourself speaking on the DVD-ROM.

Answers
1 real 2 invented 3 real 4 real 5 real 6 invented

EXPLOREReading

8   Most gadgets come with an instruction manual. Do you always read the
    instructions? Why? / Why not?

9   The instructions below are for a printer. Match the instructions to the pictures.

1   Open printer cover to remove packing materials from inside.
2   Plug in power supply.
3   Turn printer on.
4   Raise paper tray. Slide paper guide to the left. Load paper.
5   Open top cover.

6   Pull tab to remove clear tape from print cartridges.
7   Insert print cartridges. Push cartridges forward until they
    click into place.
8   Close top cover.
9   Connect USB cable.

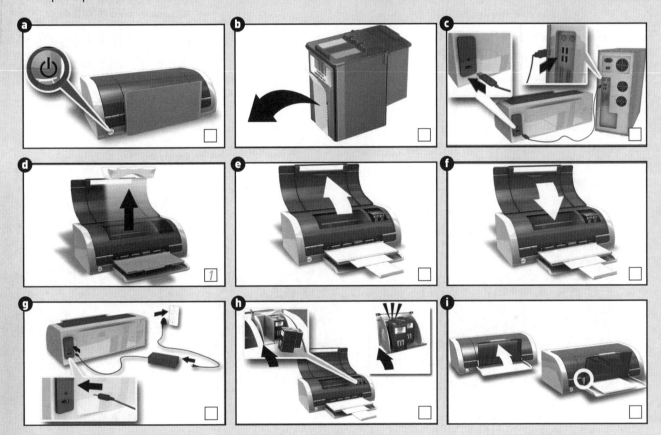

10 Choose the correct answers.

1   The instructions are written using the ...
    a   *you* form of the verb.
    b   imperative.

2   The instructions ...
    a   use articles (*a*, *an*, *the*).
    b   don't use articles (*a*, *an*, *the*).

11 Find verbs in the instructions with the following meanings.

1   to take something away   *remove*
2   to put something into something else   _____
3   to make something move smoothly over a surface _____
4   to lift something to a higher position   _____
5   to connect to the electricity   _____
6   to make a short, sharp sound   _____

12 Some gadgets have instructions in different languages. Find the instructions for
    one of your gadgets. Are they in English? Read the instructions and look up any
    words that you don't know.

1   Before you watch, think about something you learned when you were younger or an activity you used to do. How much can you remember about it?

2   Watch Mainda and Ian talking about a memory from when they were younger. Answer the questions by writing M (Mainda), I (Ian) or M/I (Mainda and Ian).

     1   Who was younger in the memory they describe?   _____

     2   Whose memory involved other people?   _____

     3   Whose memory involved sport or a game?   _____

Mainda

3   Watch Mainda again (00:11–01:03) and circle the correct answers.

     1   Mainda started learning English when she went to nursery school / primary school.

     2   She knew a couple of / no English words when she started.

     3   She understood / didn't understand what the other children were saying.

     4   She thought speaking English was a kind of game / interesting.

     5   She knows / doesn't know when she started to actually speak English.

4   Mainda uses several phrasal verbs in her story. Phrasal verbs are verbs with more than one part. Match the phrasal verbs in bold (1–4) with their meanings (a–d).

Ian

     1   When I **turned up** at the playground I ...   a   became involved in

     2   ... and made any sound you could **come up with**.   b   arrived

     3   So I **joined in** the game and ...   c   continued

     4   ... so I **carried on** ...   d   invent

5   Watch Ian again (01:09–02:02). Label the things in Ian's story with the words in the box.

> flippers   seal   wave

1 _____   2 _____   3 _____

6   Complete this sentence. Then watch the beginning of Ian's video (01:09–01:22) to check.

When I was a teenager, I lived in Cornwall. And I had to leave Cornwall to go to London to go to university.

I _____ _____ love surfing in Cornwall, so I went to the beach for one last surf.

7   Could you replace the missing words in Exercise 6 with *would*? Why? / Why not?

8   Write about a memory you have from when you were younger.

GLOSSARY

nursery school (noun): a school for very young children
Cornwall (noun): an area in the south-west of England
ride (**rode**, **ridden**) (verb): to travel on something, usually a bike; Ian uses it to talk about waves
incredible (adjective): very good or exciting
look like (verb): to seem; to have the appearance of

14 A matter of opinion

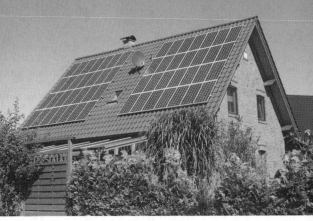

1 Look at Lewis and Amelia's opinions about boxing again (CB page 115).
There is one wrong word in each of these sentences. replace them with the words
in the box.

> anyway   course   feel   find   is   know   thing   ~~think~~

~~think~~

1   I feel it's awful.

2   I know it quite exciting.

3   We all find that people are aggressive.

4   And anyone, nobody has to box.

5   I really know that if people want to box, we shouldn't stop them.

6   Of sure that's not the same.

7   The thing was, they have rules and there's a referee.

8   Another think is, being a boxer is a job, you know.

VOCABULARY
Responding to opinions

2 Read the conversation. Is Behrang agreeing (A), disagreeing (D) or finishing what he's saying (F)?

1 JENNIFER Trying to reduce your carbon footprint is just a waste of time.
BEHRANG Sorry, but it's not a waste of time. If we all made an effort to reduce our carbon footprint, it would make a massive difference. [D]

2 JENNIFER I already do my part: I recycle and turn lights off when I'm not in the room. That's enough, isn't it?
BEHRANG Yes, but there's so much more you could do, don't you think? ☐

3 JENNIFER It all comes down to the same point: people are just too selfish to change their ways in order to help their environment.
BEHRANG Well, not really. I think it depends on the person and the information they have. ☐

4 JENNIFER Yes, but—
BEHRANG Just a second. The thing is, people need to understand that they can make a difference. ☐

5 JENNIFER But one person can't make a difference: governments need to act, too.
BEHRANG OK, that's a good point. ☐

6 JENNIFER And if governments act, then the people will follow.
BEHRANG Yes, exactly. ☐

3 Write responses to the following opinions using expressions from Exercise 2.

1 I think the government should be doing more to help the environment.

_____

2 Supermarkets are by far the best place to buy food.

_____

3 I still think banks are the safest place to keep your money.

_____

4 Going to the gym is a waste of time and money.

_____

5 Companies should stop people from using the Internet at work for personal use.

_____

GRAMMAR
Unreal conditionals

4 Eight people are discussing ideas for reducing their carbon footprints on an online forum. Complete the suggestions with the correct form of the verbs in brackets.

1 Nadine
If everyone _turned_ (turn) their heating down by 1°C, we'd save so much energy.

2 Jessica
If we charge higher taxes on air travel, people _____ (not fly) as much.

3 Leigh
If we tried to buy more local products, we _____ (reduce) the amount of food miles – the distance that food travels between the field and the shop.

4 Rahul
If we all _____ (walk) more and _____ (drive) less, we'd all reduce our carbon footprints.

5 Stefan
If more people were allowed to work from home, it _____ (reduce) the amount of traffic on the roads; fewer commuters means fewer cars.

6 Pedro
If the government invested more money in public transport, people _____ (not need) to drive as much.

7 Siga
If you _____ (buy) more second-hand products, you'll save money and help reduce your carbon footprint.

8 Aimee
If the price of oil continues to rise, the government _____ (have to) invest in new energy sources.

Over to you

Which of the ideas in Exercise 4 do you agree with? Which do you disagree with? Explain why. Record yourself speaking on the DVD-ROM.

5   Who thinks their suggestion is possible (P)? Who thinks their suggestion is imaginary and probably won't happen (I)?

1   Nadine ___/___   5   Stefan _____
2   Jessica _____   6   Pedro _____
3   Leigh _____   7   Siga _____
4   Rahul _____   8   Aimee _____

MYEnglish

6   Look at these conversations. Is the second speaker agreeing (A), disagreeing (D) or neither (N)? Don't check your answers in the key yet.

❶
A   People just aren't doing enough to reduce their own carbon footprints.
B   No, I see what you mean. ☐

❷
A   People just aren't doing enough to reduce their own carbon footprints.
C   Yes, I definitely agree. But I think most people probably are in fact doing a lot to reduce their own carbon footprints. ☐

❸
A   People just aren't doing enough to reduce their own carbon footprints.
D   Yeah, go on. ☐
A   You know, we need to be doing more.

❹
A   People just aren't doing enough to reduce their own carbon footprints.
E   Yeah, I know. ☐

❺
A   People just aren't doing enough to reduce their own carbon footprints.
F   Yes, it's true that most people aren't doing enough – that's obvious. But at the same time lots of people *are* making an effort. We just need to give people more encouragement. ☐

7   Agreeing and disagreeing is sometimes done differently in different cultures. Match the conversations in Exercise 6 (1–5) with these examples (a–e).

a   For an American, *Yeah* can mean 'I agree with you'.   [4]
b   For an American, *Yeah* can mean 'I follow you'.   ☐
c   In Burundi, it's not unusual for people to say that they agree with you, and then give an opinion that is the exact opposite.   ☐
d   In India, people sometimes say *no* and then agree with what you have just said.   ☐
e   In Japan, people will often include both sides of the argument in their response.   ☐

8   Do Exercise 6 again. Do you want to change your answers?

Your English

9   Think about these questions.

1   How do people agree and disagree in your country? Is it always clear whether someone is agreeing with you or not?
2   Can you agree and disagree in the same way in English? Would people understand you?
3   In some cultures, it is normal to disagree with people in a very direct way. Is that the case in your culture? What problems might that create when speaking English?

EXPLOREWriting

10   Look at the extract on the opposite page, from a website against the expansion of Sandstown Airport. What is the website asking you to do?

    a   write to the management of Sandstown Airport
    b   write to the press
    c   write to the government
    d   write to all three of the above

11   Ben is a local government employee. He has just been to a meeting at Sibley Town Hall. The plan is to make the local airport, Sandstown Airport, bigger. Look at his notes on the opposite page describing what local residents said about the options that were discussed at the meeting.

12   You have decided to write a letter to your local newspaper, giving your opinion on the Sandstown Airport situation. Before you write, make notes about the following questions.

    1   What do you think about the expansion of Sandstown Airport? Should it be made bigger? moved to Sibley? moved to the Nature Reserve?

    _____
    _____
    _____

    2   What two main points would you like to include in your letter/email?

    _____
    _____
    _____

    3   How can you justify your points? That is, what arguments can you use to make your points stronger?

    _____
    _____
    _____

    4   What do you think needs to be done next? Who is responsible?

    _____
    _____
    _____

13   Look at these expressions, which could all be used in your letter/email. Match the expressions (1–8) to when you would use them (a–d).

    1   The main reason for this is ...   ☐ *b*
    2   I am writing to ...   ☐
    3   We / The government / Sandstown Airport need(s) to ...   ☐
    4   If we don't ..., ... will happen.   ☐
    5   The first/second/main point I would like to make is this: ...   ☐
    6   It is clear/obvious that ...   ☐
    7   What is needed is ...   ☐
    8   According to ... , ...   ☐

    a   to explain why you are writing
    b   to justify or support your argument (x4)
    c   to say what needs to be done next and who is responsible (x2)
    d   to make your point(s)

14   Write your letter/email, following the notes you made in Exercise 12. Try to use some of the expressions in Exercise 13 and follow the advice on the website.

www.sandstownairportexpansion.com

What can you do to help?

Do you feel strongly about the expansion of Sandstown Airport? Do you think you could put pen to paper or fingers to keyboard? Well, we'd like to encourage you. After all, the more column inches the better, as far as the Sandstown Airport expansion is concerned.

Many of us read the letters pages of the newspaper as well as the articles, so it can be an excellent place to get your message across. However, getting your letter published isn't always easy. To help you, try following this advice:

* Keep your letter/email short. Not many newspapers will publish anything over 250 words.
* Try to include only one or two main points; it will help you keep your letter/email short and direct.
* Start the letter/email with a summary of your main points in one or two sentences.
* In the next section, go into more details, giving reasons for your opinions.
* Finish by saying what you think needs to be done next and who is responsible.

Sounds easy, doesn't it? Why don't you give it a go!

---

1 Make the airport that is already in Sandstown bigger
+ There is already part of the airport there, so it's a good idea to continue to build in the same space.
- The roads near Sandstown are small, and more traffic will cause problems for local people and people travelling to the airport.

2 Move the airport to Sibley
+ Sibley has enough roads to deal with the extra people travelling to the airport.
- Sibley is a peaceful, quiet town that needs people to visit it. Most people work in the tourist industry. The airport could mean that people won't want to visit the town.

3 Build on the Nature Reserve
+ This will keep the people in Sandstown and Sibley happy - neither of the towns will suffer from making the airport bigger.
- A lot of unusual birds and animals will lose their natural habitat and will have nowhere to live.

1   In their free time, Amanda is a local politician and Claire practises a martial art. Before you watch, think about these questions: do you do, or have you ever thought about doing, these things? Can you imagine any problems that they have had?

2   Watch Amanda and Claire and choose the best summary for each person.

Amanda

Claire

a   Amanda is a local politician. She sometimes finds it hard to make everybody happy.

b   Amanda is a local politician. She sometimes finds it hard to make young people happy.

a   Claire always wanted to do martial arts, but never did.

b   Claire always wanted to do martial arts and is now very good at it.

3   Watch again. Are the sentences true or false?

Amanda

1   As a local politician, Amanda has to talk to local people and other politicians.   TRUE / FALSE
2   There is a park in the area Amanda looks after.   TRUE / FALSE
3   The people who live near the park have the same opinion as the young people who use the park.   TRUE / FALSE

Claire

4   Claire liked doing dance and gymnastics when she was younger.   TRUE / FALSE
5   Claire started to do a martial art when she was seven.   TRUE / FALSE
6   Claire is now a black belt.   TRUE / FALSE

4   Some verbs in English often go with the same words. For example, we say *have lunch* not *take lunch*. This is called a 'collocation'. If a word 'collocates' with another word, it often goes with it. Match the verbs (1–7) with the words they collocate with (a–g).

1   do   a   gymnastics
2   take   b   a debate
3   do   c   with (someone)
4   have   d   a martial art
5   disagree   e   decisions
6   give   f   (someone) a hard time
7   look   g   after

5   Watch again and complete the extracts from the video with the correct form of the collocations from Exercise 4.

1   ... we consider proposals, _____ and then we _____ .
2   For example, we have a lovely big park in the area I _____ .
3   I've always wanted to _____ .
4   ... I didn't want to _____ .
5   ... it's not a girl thing and so they totally _____ me.
6   Someone _____ me _____ and upset me a lot so I went to my parents ...

6   Do you have any opinions about issues in your local area? What are they?

GLOSSARY

black belt (noun): If you have a **black belt** in a martial art, you are at a high level of it.
disturbance (noun): something that interrupts what you are doing
martial art (noun): *Karate* and *judo* are examples of **martial arts**.
politician (noun): a person who works in politics
proposals (plural noun): suggestions
recreation (noun): things you do for fun

Acknowledgements

The authors would like to thank the editorial team in Cambridge, particularly Greg Sibley and Neil Holloway. Many thanks also to Catriona Watson-Brown for her ever-thorough copy-editing.

Maggie Baigent would like to thank Michael Cotton for his loyalty and support.

Chris Cavey would like to thank Kate, Lily and Ella for their patience and support.

Nick Robinson would like to thank Anna Barnard.

The authors and publishers are also grateful to the following contributors:

Text design and page make-up: Stephanie White at Kamae Design
Picture research: Hilary Luckcock

The authors and publishers acknowledge the following sources of copyright material and are grateful for the permissions granted. While every effort has been made, it has not always been possible to identify the sources of all the material used, or to trace all copyright holders. If any omissions are brought to our notice, we will be happy to include the appropriate acknowledgements on reprinting.

For the text on p. 7: © Copyright University of Glamorgan 2008–2009. All rights reserved; for the text on p. 27: Reproduced with permission from the Lonely Planet Website www.lonelyplanet.com © 2009 Lonely Planet Publications Pty Ltd; for the text on p. 37: © Simon Calder, the *Independent*, 2nd August 2008.

The publisher has used its best endeavours to ensure that the URLs for external websites referred to in this book are correct and active at the time of going to press. However, the publisher has no responsibility for the websites and can make no guarantee that a site will remain live or that the content is or will remain appropriate.

The publishers are grateful to the following for the permissions to reproduce copyright photographs and material:

Key: l = left, c = centre, r = right, t = top, b = bottom

Alamy/©ImageState for p4(tc), /©SuperStock for p4(bc), /©Alex Segre for p4(c), /©blickwinkel for p11(r), /©Elizabeth Whiting & Associates for p14(t), /©imagebroker for p16(8), /©i love images for p17(l), /©PhotosIndia.com LLC for p17(c), /©Emilio Ereza for p20, /©Blend Images for p21(tl), /©Image Source Black for p21(tr), /©Diffused Productions for p21(bl), /©Chris Rout for p21(br), /©Shoosmith Railway Collection for p24(l), /©imagebroker for p24(c), /©Derek Askill for p25(t), /©Leslie Garland Picture Library for p32, /©Frank Chmura for p36, /©International Photobank for p37, /©Vintage Image for p41(c), /©Adrian Sherratt for p57, /©Jon Arnold Images for p59(br), /©Phil Degginger for p59(tr), /©Hola Images for p61(tcr), /©Peter Arnold Inc for p61(bc), /©David J Green-Lifestyle for p65(b), /©John Miller for p69(cl); Corbis/©Bernardo Bucci for p10(l), /©Turbo for p40(b), /©flame for p44(7), /©Eric Cahan for p52(t), /©Barry Rosenthal for p55(t), /©Image Source for p69(tl), /©Shawn Frederick for p69(b); Fears and Kahn for 40(tl, tc, tr); Getty Images/©Win-Initiative for p11(l), /©Photographer's Choice for p41(t), /©PhotoDisc for p44(1), /©Hulton Archive for p61(t), /©Hisham Ibrahim for p61(cl), /©Charlie Schuck for p69(tr), /©Simon Watson for p70; istockphoto/©Stephanie Swartz for p9(2), /©Brad Wieland for p9(3), /©Dawn Liljenquist for p9(4), /©Radu Razvan for p9(5), /©Amanda Krishnan for p21(bc), /©Tom Hahn for p25(b), /©Steve Geer for p45, /©Simone van den Berg for p46(t), /©mamahoohooba for p46(ct), /©Liza McCorkie for p46(cb), /©TommL for p46(b), /©Ana Vasileva for p51(b), /©Thorsten Rust for p54(b), /©Linda & Colin McKie for p59(bl), /©Juergen Bosse for p60(t), /©ad_doward for p61(cr);   Lebrecht Music & Arts/©Martin Thompson for p4(tr), 4(br); Masterfile/©Chad Johnston for p10(r); Photolibrary/©Thinkstock for p9(1), /©Joel Sartore for p11(c), /©Comstock for p15, /©fancy for p17(r), /©Sylvain Grandadam for p19, /©Olive Images for p24(r), /©Digital Vision for p44(2), /©Digital Vision for p44(5), /©Digital Vision for p44(6), /©White for p44(8), /©Thinkstock for p49, /©Blend Images for p51(t), /©Liat Chen for p55(b), /©Jeff Greenberg for p65(t); Pictures Colour Library/©George Munday for p4(br), /©Intervision Ltd for p14(b); Punchstock/©Digital Vision for p14(l), /©Cultura for p31; Rex Features/©Ben Alcraft for p39, /©Sipa Press for p60(b); Shutterstock/©Timurpix for p4(tl), /©Ales Nowak for p6, /©Phil Date for p9(6), /©Karin Lau for p9(7), /©gpalmer for p9(8), /©ZTS for p16(1), /©vinicius Tupinamba for p16(2), /©luchschen for p16(3), /©Kentoh for p16(4), /©Anton Gvozdikov for p16(5), /©Chin Kit Sen for p16(6), /©Juha-Pekka Kervinen for p16(7), /©stoupa for p16(9), /©Robert Redelowski for p16(10), /©iNNOCENt for p18(tr), /©Aki Jinn for p18(br), /©Johnathan Esper for p33, /©Galyna Andrushko for p44(3), /©Photosani for p44(4), /©Chepko Danil Vitarevich for p52(b), /©Pichugin Dmitry for p59(tl), /©yurok for p59(tc), /©Juriah Mosin for p61(cc), /©Jeff Gynane for p61(br), /©Shi Yali for p61(bl), /©ene for p64(tl), /©Jaroslaw Grudzvinski for p64(tr), /©Chunni4691 for p64(br), /©Planner for p64(tc), /©Jessmine for p64(bl), /©Eric Gevaert for p68(bl), /©VeF for p68(bc), /©objectsforall for p68(br), /©Otmar Smit for p69(cr), /©Soundsnaps for p73(r), /©Mark William Richardson for p73(l).

Illustrations by Tom Croft, Mark Duffin, Kamae Design, Julian Mosedale, Nigel Sanderson, Martin Sanders